MUSIC AND THE MODERNS

The Life and Works of Carol Robinson

by
GLENDA DAWN GOSS

The Scarecrow Press, Inc.
Metuchen, N.J., & London
1993

Frontispiece: Carol Robinson. Silverpoint drawing by Joseph Stella. From the Carol Robinson Collection, Hargrett Rare Book and Manuscript Library, University of Georgia. Reprinted by permission.

British Library Cataloguing-in-Publication data available

Library of Congress Cataloging-in-Publication Data

Goss, Glenda Dawn.
  Music and the moderns : the life and works of Carol Robinson / by Glenda Dawn Goss.
     p. cm.
  Includes bibliographical references and index.
  ISBN 0-8108-2626-7 (acid-free paper)
  1. Robinson, Carol, 1889-1979.   2.   Pianists--United States-- Biography. I. Title.
ML417.R65G67 1993
786.2'092--dc20
[B]
                                                            92-37179

To Jean Réti-Forbes

TABLE OF CONTENTS

ACKNOWLEDGMENTS

The present book is neither a dissertation nor the realization of a lifetime dream. I never intended to write about Carol Robinson for the simple reason that, until four years ago, I had never heard of her. Then one day a I received a request from a Soviet scholar for a copy of the *Jazz Sonata* by George Antheil. Sure that no such manuscript existed in our library, I discovered to my astonishment not only Antheil's holograph but a unique work by Bohuslav Martinů and copies of Charles Ives's manuscripts, all among the papers of a Carol Robinson. "Who was Carol Robinson?" I naturally asked. No one, it seemed, really knew.

Carol Robinson's papers themselves provided some clues. Yet these disconnected clippings, programs, teaching notes, and music manuscripts raised more questions than they answered. Why did Antheil inscribe his delightful *Sonata* to this obscure pianist? How did she come to own a keyboard work of Czech composer Martinů that was completely unknown in today's musical world? What were those photostatic copies of Charles Ives's *Second* and *Third Piano and Violin Sonatas* doing among her possessions? No music reference source, not even the newer ones devoted to women, helped with any of these questions. Eventually, I found a brief entry for Robinson in *Women of Achievement* (New York: House of Field, 1940). There and in the *Leschetizky Bulletins* of the 1950s she was clearly recognized as a leader. But these materials, which hardly justified so much as a short article, did not begin to satisfy my curiosity. The library seemed unyielding.

Trained as a Renaissance scholar in the 1970s school of American musicology with its goals of diligent archival research to reconstruct a biographical picture and painstaking critical commentary to fashion a musical edition, I gradually realized I would have to develop some new methods if I wanted my questions answered. It was, appropriately enough, through post-Renaissance technology—the telephone—that I finally began to unravel the Gordian knot of Carol Robinson's life in music. Making call after call, I came closer and closer to Robinson's intimate circle, first to acquaintances, then to friends and pupils, and finally, in response to a last-ditch advertisement in a Plattsburg, New York, newspaper, to Carol Robinson's nephew and niece. These real-life conversations, which I had held only in imagination (or in nightmares) with my Renaissance characters, constitute an essential source of information about Robinson and her time. Through them I learned of her involvement with the exotic Gurdjieff, to which written allusions are

vii

virtually non-existent. I began to uncover her connections to Olgivanna and Frank Lloyd Wright, only hinted at in the *Leschetizky Bulletins*. I was told of her friendship with Margaret Anderson and Jane Heap, a revelation that sent me scurrying to *The Little Review*. Sure enough, in its pages Carol lives in full-page advertisements side by side with articles and iconography by her friends—Antheil, Hemingway, Pound, Man Ray, H.D. (Hilda Doolittle), Pavel Tchelichev, Fernand Leger, Mary Garden. As family and friends began sending their recollections together with additional letters, photographs, clippings, and finally, her music, the image of a remarkable person came more and more clearly into focus, that of a woman of enormous musical talent who eschewed worldly fame for the greater challenges of self-discovery and self-development. More than anything else, it was the depth of Carol Robinson's twentieth-century experience and her determination to live her life on a higher plane that convinced me her story should be told.

I owe then an unusually great debt to the many individuals who so freely responded to my telephone calls, my letters, and my visits; it is a pleasure to acknowledge them here. Many of their names appear in the "Interviews and Correspondence" section of the Bibliography, and I thank them all for their time and their willingness to reflect on Carol Robinson and her times. In particular I wish to acknowledge Robinson's family, David Robinson and Phoebe Sells, for entrusting me with precious photographs, tapes, and other treasured family materials, and for allowing me to publish her music. Robinson's gifted pupil, Julie Steinberg, and her mother Millie, put themselves often at my disposal and provided copies of most of Robinson's music. Elizabeth Delza has been a constant source of valuable information and useful documents, but even more, of support and inspiration. Her own extraordinary life deserves a telling. The staff at the Library of Congress Music Division and Kendall Crilley of Yale's John Gerrick Jackson Music Library together with Charles Amirkhanian of the Antheil Estate and Hjordis Halvorson of Chicago's Newberry Library graciously provided copies of documents, answers to questions, and access to collections. I should like to thank Charles Amirkhanian for permission to reproduce the Antheil manuscript and correspondence included here; Lucy Forbes Shevenell for permission to examine the Réti-Forbes papers; and Wayne Shirley, who provided a detailed account of a recent Antheil concert in Carnegie Hall and made valuable suggestions about the Antheil chapter. For permission to publish this chapter, which appears as "George Antheil, Carol Robinson, and *The Little Review* Circle" in the Winter 1993 issue of *American Music*, I thank the University of Illinois Press. I would like to express my gratitude also to the University of Georgia Research Foundation for support provided during the final phase of the project.

At the University of Georgia, various individuals in the School of Music were vital to this research. It was Roger Dancz, jazz professor, who first drew my attention to the Carol Robinson Collection and Harriet Hair and Charlotte Reinke who suggested the New York contacts that finally broke the logjam about Carol Robinson's identity. Alan Houtchens verified Bohuslav Martinů's hand and patiently translated the articles in Czech I brought to him. There are also the staff members of the University of Georgia Libraries, who cannot be praised too highly. Despite my repeated and often complicated requests, Susan Morris and her Interlibrary Loan Department always responded with good humor and the requested source. In the Music Division, Bill Coscarelli and his staff cheerfully assisted in ways too numerous to mention. And the staff members of the Hargrett Library are every scholar's dream. I wish to thank especially Mary Ellen Brooks, Nelson Morgan, and Larry Gulley, whose enthusiasm and interest often buoyed me when mine flagged. One and all, these individuals deserve new computers with multiple data indexes—or whatever heavenly rewards most befit hardworking librarians. Finally, without the help of LaMurl Morris, my longsuffering typist, Suzanne Gilbert, who carefully proofread the manuscript and prepared the index, and Tim Waters, who prepared the music, this book would have remained a manuscript.

ABBREVIATIONS

CC=Carbon Copy

GU=University of Georgia, Hargrett Rare Book and Manuscript Library,
Athens, Georgia

LAA=Leschetizky Association of America

LC=Library of Congress, Music Division, Washington, D.C.

LS=Letter Signed by

LIST OF MUSIC EXAMPLES

George Antheil, *Jazz Sonata*, title page and dedication and the opening mm. 1-12, Example 7, pp. 61-62.

George Antheil, *Jazz Sonata*, mm. 26-36, Example 8, pp. 65-66.

George Antheil, *Jazz Symphony*, rehearsal no. 36, Example 9, p. 67.

George Antheil, *Jazz Symphony*, 4 mm. before rehearsal no. 53, Example 10, p. 68.

George Antheil, *Jazz Symphony*, revised version, rehearsal no. 2, Example 11, p. 71.

Bohuslav Martinů, *Par T.S.F.*, mm. 1-18, Example 12, p. 88.

Carol Robinson, *Shadowy Woodlands*, mm. 1-6, Example 1, p. 30.

Carol Robinson, *The Moon Was But a Chin of Gold*, mm. 1-4, Example 2, p. 32.

Carol Robinson, *Velvet Shoes*, mm. 1-4, Example 3, p. 34.

Carol Robinson, *Never More Will the Wind*, mm. 1-4, Example 4, p. 35.

Carol Robinson, *Pedagogical Exercise No. 4*, Example 5, pp. 37-38.

Carol Robinson, *Chorale Dance for Elizabeth Delza*, mm. 1-18, Example 6, p. 42.

LIST OF PROGRAMS

A Dance Recital of Modern Music by Henri and Carol Robinson, Pianist, Program 1, pp. 13-15.

Afternoon musicales with the Bechstein Pianoforte, Program 2, pp. 16-17.

Modern Music: Carol Robinson, Program 3, pp. 19-20.

Dance Recital, Elizabeth Delza, Program 4, p. 41.

The Little Review's Advertisement for the Steinert Piano, featuring Carol Robinson, Program 5, p. 57.

League of Composers, First Lecture-Recital, Program 6, p. 63.

George Antheil, Carnegie Hall Concert, Program 7, p. 69.

Pro-Musica, Second Referendum Concert, Program 8, pp. 73-74.

The Maverick Sunday Concerts, Program 9, p. 83.

Elizabeth Delza with Dance Group, Program 10, pp. 85-86.

Contemporary American Program, Program 11, p. 92.

PREFACE

A notice from Margaret Anderson and Jane Heap of *The Little Review* informed us about a piano concert of all modern music to be given by a remarkable young American artist, Carol Robinson—a discovery. This was in the early 'twenties.

In those days, my husband Gorham Munson and I followed the modern scene avidly in all the arts—he particularly in literature, and I especially in music and dance. Of course, we went eagerly to this concert.

Carol Robinson's playing was awakening. Her style was original, strong, yet subtle, and the music on the program invigorating.

It was later when I made acquaintance with Carol Robinson that I discovered the personality just as original as the piano style, and the quality of the person arresting and engaging. She had a simple elegance of bearing, an easy, informal formality, with the appearance of a friendly reserve. Her conversation was alive and tinged with wit; her talk of musicians and anecdotes enchanting and sometimes hilarious.

When I knew her well, she had already been playing as soloist with the major orchestras in this country and was teaching many talented pupils. Many concert tours followed. In 1927 George Antheil's *Ballet mécanique* came to Carnegie Hall in New York with much advance publicity. There were four pianos on stage, other instruments and noninstruments like a real propeller and machine-made noise to create sounds of modern life. Carol Robinson was one of the pianists; Aaron Copland, another.

Antheil later complained that everything was wrongly arranged. The critics had a field day—as did many in the audience—but many of us were gratefully excited by the daring, the energy.

Carol's involvement with music brought her to Paris often to work with Nadia Boulanger and Wanda Landowska and to meet young musicians and composers of the period. One of these was Bohuslav Martinů who presented her with his manuscript of his delightful *Par T.S.F.*

As a teacher, Carol Robinson always remembered her famous teacher, Fannie Bloomfield Zeisler, who had inspired her and made her assistant teacher at an early age. But Carol brought to her own teaching the originality and perception that had impressed me at her early concert. Her originality was not only in the technique of playing, but in the method she evolved to reach and develop each individual essentially. Her method included group-sessions in ear-training, theory, harmony and studies of different styles of various composers. She played examples of such elements on the piano, to the delight and enchantment of the group. In these ways, she developed a musicality in each pupil from the variety of the music they played and heard. Even the youngest loved Bartók as they did Mozart or Schumann.

Carol Robinson's interest in all the arts and her preoccupation with her own development gave her a unique way of communicating and drawing out a remarkable response from her pupils which helped make them true musical artists. Her teaching was greatly appreciated in several colleges, and, of course, her long affiliation with the Dalcroze School is well known.

Carol Robinson always brought something fresh to her work and her life. First and foremost she was a natural musician. Music lived in her—her great musical scholarship was without ostentation, but impressive. Her inner ear was quick and sensitive to sound in every subtle aspect. Not only her ear, but her eye could detect the slightest error. And her candor could be surprising, as in the case of a piano recital in which she shouted from the audience "Awful!" and walked out. She had no hesitancy in producing shock if a talented pupil showed repeated neglect. Sometimes it was dismissal. But this was rare. Integrity may be a suitable way to describe Carol's musicality as well as her way of life. Her development grew with the Gurdjieff influence. It made her realize that the inevitable concert tours, pleasurable and gratifying as they were, did not lead to her aims for herself. So she gradually withdrew from a life of touring and devoted herself to making her kind of teaching her primary work, while giving occasional performances and doing some composing.

Many performances were given at Taliesen at the invitation of Olgivanna and Frank Lloyd Wright who were devoted friends and admirers of Carol. Among other special friends were Sidney and Henry Cowell and the concert pianist Ralph Lawton. It was Carol Robinson and Ralph Lawton who introduced me to Katherine Ruth Heyman and her Skryabin circle. And it was again Carol Robinson and Ralph Lawton, director of *Music and Art* on Cape Cod, who did me the honor of playing for my Dance Concert on Cape Cod. And it was Carol herself who played for my Dance Concert in Washington when we introduced for the first time four dances to music of G.I. Gurdjieff (then unpublished), which Carol played with such understanding and distinction. Our collaboration in this venture came from our mutual interest in the music, in the dance, in the approach.

Carol Robinson had a delightful way of sharing music with friends by inviting them as guests to special concerts. Or, when very ill at the end when she could not share the outer world of music, she made a habit of presenting gifts of tickets for special concerts, be it Prokofiev, Bartók, Berio, Ives, Messiaen, Beethoven, Bach. . .

In this way, she had joy and gave joy. Carol Robinson and music were synonymous.

Elizabeth Delza

INTRODUCTION

Carol Robinson, born in 1889, lived a long and exceptionally full life as an outstanding pianist, a gifted teacher, and an occasional composer. Until her death in 1979, she befriended and encouraged her avant-garde contemporaries, often working closely with the artists, philosophers, writers, dancers, musicians, and composers whose creative activities shaped the intellectual life of the twentieth century. Her personal strengths and disciplined musicianship endeared her to students. Her sensitive interpretations of contemporary music repeatedly earned critical acclaim. Her friendships with George Antheil, Bohuslav Martinů, and Henry Cowell led her to première their music. Prompted by her own inclinations, she championed *Les Six*, Stravinsky, Debussy, Bartók, Skryabin, and Satie across the United States.

Despite such clear contributions to America's musical life, the name Carol Robinson does not appear in any standard reference. One reason probably has to do with Carol herself; she lacked "that quality of vanity," as one friend observed, to promote herself in the musical world. Another recalled that she also lacked the money required to keep up a musical social life. Unable to afford the price of a reputation, she eventually devoted herself almost entirely to teaching, a profession for which she was eminently gifted. That scholars traditionally pay only scant attention even to the most dedicated teachers and renowned performers has not helped Carol Robinson's case. Yet those who knew Robinson recognize her as extraordinary, a woman who was a leader, and not only in the experience of music, but also in the experience of being.

In this book Carol Robinson's story will be told as completely as known resources allow. This figure will thereby be given well-deserved acknowledgment and a written place in the record of events she helped to create. It is my hope that the present account, by providing a deeply sympathetic portrait of a woman who deserves to be remembered for her unique personal qualities, will show how the strengths and talents of the world's less conspicuous individuals affect the currents of music history. Carol Robinson's story also illuminates many aspects of the twentieth century that otherwise would remain obscure. By offering us a revealing and rewarding journey that strays off the beaten tracks as often as it parallels them, Robinson enables us to see contemporary music in the much richer context of American intellectual life rather than as a series of isolated musical events. By portraying something of the depth, the scope, and the continuity of that life, this book serves modern history as well as music.

Many of the primary materials necessary for writing this narrative belong to the University of Georgia. Before her death, Miss Robinson transferred her papers to the University of Georgia's Hargrett Rare Book and Manuscript Library where they rest today in four boxes classified together as MS 300. These contain recital programs, publicity materials, correspondence, news clippings, reviews, and teaching notes. A number of teaching scores, marked frequently with Robinson's personal comments, comprise a separate collection (called simply "The Robinson Collection") in the Music Reference Library of the University's School of Music. Additional correspondence reposes in the Jean Réti-Forbes Papers, MS 912, in the Hargrett Rare Book and Manuscript Library. I deeply appreciate the permission granted by Lucy Forbes Shevenell to be the first to examine these documents. The Olin Downes Papers, MS 688, also in the Hargrett Library, verify and expand upon Miss Robinson's activities, although Downes and Robinson seem to have carried on no correspondence.

Supplementing the archival materials, students, friends, family, and colleagues have come forth with memories, treasured correspondence, and their own genealogical research. To one student, today an acclaimed pianist, Miss Robinson entrusted many of her own compositions. These compositions together with other materials contributed by her friends around the world were graciously shared to benefit the present study.

A third source of information resides in the writings of Carol's contemporaries. Although Robinson, who was very reticent about her personal fortunes, did not leave any prose accounts of her life, many of her friends, from Gorham Munson to Ezra Pound, Dorothy Caruso to Margaret Anderson, George Antheil to Georgette Leblanc, left memoirs that provide valuable insights into the people and ideas of Robinson's circle. These appear in the Bibliography under "Writings by Carol Robinson's Friends."

In the following pages Carol Robinson's story will be used as a point of departure for considerations of larger issues in American-life. In Part I, her concert career demonstrates the place—both literally and figuratively—of contemporary music in America: literally, in showing how geographically widespread were her concerts of the "ultramoderns"; figuratively, in showing Americans' responses to new music in the early twentieth century. Vital ideas in American intellectual life manifest themselves in Carol Robinson's own compositions, many of which connect her to some of the most distinguished figures in art, literature, architecture, dance, and philosophy of the century.

Part II shows how the circumstances of Carol's life intertwined first with those of the notorious American composer George Antheil and next with those of Czechoslovakia's beloved Bohuslav Martinů. Works by each composer survive in rare or unique manuscripts among Robinson's papers in the Hargrett Library where they have lain virtually unknown to the musical world. Photostatic copies of Charles Ives's *Second* and *Third Piano and Violin Sonatas* also rest among the papers of this pianist who figures among Ives's earliest advocates. Appendix A lists Robinson's extensive concert repertory, showing when and where she performed each work; Appendix B presents the works she herself composed; and Appendix C enumerates the piano rolls she made.

The unlikely assortment of manuscripts by composers of the stature of Antheil, Ives, and Martinů alone makes the Carol Robinson Collection an intriguing source to study. With the added fascination of Robinson herself, through whom we come to understand other individuals and ideas of the twentieth century, her story becomes an irresistible one to write. Robinson's papers belong to the University of Georgia because of another pianist and teacher, Jean Réti-Forbes, a member of the University's Music Department during the 1960s. Widow of Serbian theorist and composer Rudolf Réti, Jean Réti-Forbes, a devoted musician and scholar, was a close friend of Carol Robinson and Olin Downes. She persuaded the University to acquire the personal papers of each. Jean died in Athens in 1972, but her legacy as a teacher and a scholar promises to enrich twentieth-century music for years to come. This book is dedicated to her memory.

PART I

THE LIFE OF CAROL ROBINSON

Carol Robinson came of age during a particularly auspicious time for women. From the very beginning of the twentieth century, American women exhibited an outlook of optimism and a spirit of adventure in leading their own lives that set them apart both from their predecessors and from their contemporaries elsewhere in the world. William O'Neill called the period between 1890 and 1920 a "kind of feminist golden age,"[1] and George H. Douglas has chronicled responses of many women who

> perceived some new quality of experience in the America of the twentieth century, and set out to analyze, to celebrate, to criticize, even to exploit, a freshly unfolding facet of the cultural experience. They wrote, they flew, they danced, they preached—in short, they *performed* their insights and made public their own experience.[2]

One of these remarkable, performing individualists, Carol Robinson in a certain sense stands for all. Her unquenchable curiosity about the new in art, her enthusiastic championship of contemporary music, her courageous turn from the pursuit of worldly fame to a life of spiritual depth illustrate the kind of gutsy living found in other heroic figures of her time, from Amelia Earhart to Martha Graham, Edna St. Vincent Millay to Dorothy Parker, Emma Goldman to Jane Addams. Because the sources of her strength stem from her background as well as from the time and place in which she was born, it will be to her childhood and youth that we first turn.

NOTES

1. William L. O'Neill, *The Woman Movement, Feminism in the United States and England* (London: George Allen and Unwin, 1969), p. 73.

2. George H. Douglas, *Women of the 20s* (Dallas, Texas: W.W. Norton, 1986), p. 15.

CHAPTER 1

CAROL ROBINSON, PIANIST

The story of Carol Robinson begins in rural mid-America. Born in Greenville, Illinois, November 26, 1889, Carol came into a family of educated, free-thinking parents who encouraged their daughter's early musical talents and intellectual capacity to an unusual degree. The Robinsons seemed to have made no gender distinctions in the expectations or the education of their two girls and two boys. The father, William Ernest Robinson (1857-1936), of Scotch-Irish descent, believed education to be the key to individual freedom. He pursued his own formal instruction through two years at Illinois Industrial University; after his four children had grown, he returned to school himself to finish a college degree. In the interim he served for a time as County School Superintendent. "A more systematic man never held office," declared the *Greenville Advocate*, which singled out for particular praise the circulating libraries, the uniform textbooks, and the system of county-wide examinations that Robinson had established.[1] Meanwhile, Robinson provided for his family by such prudent and scientific management of his farmland that he set new standards for accuracy and operations in the poultry industry.[2]

Although William Ernest played the dulcimer, the musician in the family was unequivocally Carol's mother, Clara O. White (1857-1939). One family member recalls that when it became apparent the child Carol had serious musical interests, William Ernest Robinson "turned the raising of her entirely over to her mother."[3] A more valuable example for Carol and her sister to emulate would be hard to imagine.

Born on a farm like her husband, Clara White had also pursued a higher education, far less common among women than among men of her generation. Encouraged by her family, who had come by covered wagon to Illinois with their beloved hymn books, Clara spent two years at Francis Shimer College and then left for Boston to study voice, speech, and drama. Upon her return, Clara taught voice and piano at Almira, a school that later became Greenville College. After marrying William Ernest in 1884, she not only raised four children, but also taught piano and took an active part in Illinois' cultural life. When the family moved to Springfield, she founded the Morning Etude musical club and became its first President; she frequently lectured at the quarterly meetings of the Bond County School Association; notably, she marched on behalf of women's suffrage, an endeavor in which she enjoyed her husband's

5

support.[4] Clara White led the way into an age of reform for women that began in 1890 (and that was recently commemorated in the Smithsonian National Museum in the exhibit "From Parlor to Politics: Women and Reform in America, 1890-1925"). Remembered as "more the gentle persuader of the two parents," Clara profoundly shaped her daughter's outlook.

A clipping from her mother that Carol saved gives the directions that Carol herself followed:

Aspire to do great things; then do great things . . .
Crowd all the useful beauty into your life you can possibly stow away . . .
Read, read, read, but read understandingly, without unhealthy scepticism. . .
Hold your ideals in the clouds . . .
Picture to yourself daily the type of personality you aspire to possess . . .
Above all things, have faith in the best . . .
Do these things and your musical personality with proper attention to your art will develop to a far greater state of effectiveness than could be possible through mere music study with the greatest masters on earth.[5]

The high-minded ideals that set the tone for many American women in the twentieth century formed a basic part also of Carol Robinson's early life.

Carol Robinson grew up without the burden that women should subordinate themselves, and not surprisingly, both she and her older sister (named Clara after the mother) fulfilled their early potential, Carol as a musician, Clara as an English professor. In later years Carol reflected back this openness to people and ideas and the love of learning that both parents had fostered, for she encouraged her niece and nephew and great nieces and nephews to study in equal measure philosophy, the Bible, and teachings from the Far East, and sent them *Life* magazine articles on the Great Religions of the World.

With both parents deeply involved in education, it was perhaps inevitable that Carol's goal to become a good piano teacher should emerge early. In pursuit of this dream, Carol made her way by 1910 from Springfield to Chicago, the city Margaret Anderson described wonderingly as "enchanted ground"—for its beautiful Lake Michigan; for its Frank Lloyd Wright-designed Book Store in the Fine Arts Building on Michigan Boulevard; for its incomparable literary figures; and for its music: the symphony and Frederick Stock and Mary Garden and Fannie Bloomfield Zeisler, whom Carol Robinson sought out for study.

The redoubtable Mrs. Zeisler (1863-1927), once a student of Theodore Leschetizky (who often called her "my electric wonder"),[6] wielded far-reaching influence on Chicago's musical life. Together with her husband, a prominent lawyer, Mrs. Zeisler had "a high social position and . . . what is said to be the only 'salon' in Chicago," the *National Cyclopedia* reported in 1917.[7] In later years Carol still remembered vividly those Wednesday salons, held the last of each month, "on which the choicest spirits of Chicago have a rendezvous at their home."[8] She described them as gatherings around "a stage and two pianos, lush in the style of the period . . . festive with lights, flowers, beautiful rugs, paintings and sculpture, signed photographs of celebrities. Here a brilliant company listened to chamber music, heard distinguished guest artists and . . . gifted pupils got coveted chances to play and to sit in on conversation that ranged far and wide."[9] Carol would find—or create—similarly stimulating environments all of her life.

Mrs. Zeisler had built a reputation as one of the foremost pianists in America with "lofty idealism, unremitting industry, indomitable energy, and absolute sincerity."[10] Yet Carol discovered that she considered teaching the greatest of the arts, for the young woman's desire "to be a good piano teacher" sparked Mrs. Zeisler's well-remembered "incandescent look" and garnered her solid support.[11] Not all students responded to the frank and outspoken criticisms and the near obsession with musical matters. Mrs. Zeisler frightened away the faint-hearted and astonished even the less easily intimidated (including Margaret Anderson) with her laments that her "critical faculty never permitted her the simple pleasure of listening to music emotionally."[12] In the young woman from Springfield, however, the small, intense Fannie built morale and imparted the creative excitement of teaching. The mastery Mrs. Zeisler herself demonstrated in performance and in instruction and her formidable personal qualities equally describe the mature Carol Robinson. "Formidable!" "Just a master," Carol's students have said today in recalling her.

Robinson clearly attained her first ambition to succeed at teaching in Chicago, and at the age of 80, she was actively nurturing young pianists still. In those early years, the first mark of her teaching success came on the day recalled by fellow student Ruth Wydman Jarmie "when Carol Robinson, in class, was recognized as 'assistant,' and I vowed to direct all my energies to the same goal."[13] In the capacity of *vorbereiter* (preparatory teacher), Robinson worked with Mrs. Zeisler for seven years, administering preparatory studies and exercises to new, usually younger, students prior to their full admission to her mentor's studio. Carol Robinson seems to have felt her historical position keenly in this capacity;

a "teaching genealogy" among the papers she left with Phoebe Sells reads:
"Beethoven-Czerny-Leschetizky-F. Blomfield [sic]-Robinson."

If as hardworking assistant she relieved Mrs. Zeisler of some of
the more tedious aspects of teaching, Robinson enjoyed in return her
respected teacher's trust and also her encouragement to perform. Years
later, Carol recounted how Mrs. Zeisler accompanied her to the first
rehearsal for her debut with the Chicago Symphony.[14] Just before her
pupil went up to play, Mrs. Zeisler slipped something into her hands with
the admonition to "wear this today and tomorrow. It will bring you
luck." Miss Robinson found herself clasping the mother-of-pearl dove
Theodore Leschetizky had given young Fannie before her own first
rehearsal with the Vienna Philharmonic.

Despite some earlier shaky beginnings ("Not so very long ago Miss
Robinson gave a piano recital at Kimball Hall, during which she
committed the pardonable but regrettable artistic demeanor of memory
lapses and similar minor imperfections," worried Herman DeVries of the
Chicago Evening American[15]), this time the Chicago critics responded
warmly. DeVries noted that his

> . . . nervousness for her was dispelled after she had played
> a few lines . . . before she was half way through the first
> movement she displayed all the excellent qualities inherited
> from her master-mentor, Madame Bloomfield-Zeisler. Her
> tone is lovely in pianissimo passages and always musical in
> forte. The technic is lean, accurate, the interpretation
> intelligent and refined. At the same time one feels that she
> is not entirely the reflection of careful tuition, but that
> there is a good stratum of individual art-appreciation in her
> make-up.[16]

From Chicago, Robinson built an impressive record of performances and inspired glowing reviews. To judge from the concert and recital
programs she saved over fifty years, Robinson maintained a grueling
performance schedule throughout the second and third decades of the
century, travelling from coast to coast and also from continent to
continent. Her nephew recalls that she often took the Flying Tigers
freight line, sandwiched between refrigerators as she flew from Illinois to
Missouri to Texas to Washington and Oregon.[17]

The year 1924 represents well enough these years of her life. She
began the year in Medford, Oregon, giving a recital a week in the
Northwest; by February, she had crossed the continent to play with the
Boston Symphony Orchestra in Providence, Rhode Island; in Boston the
following week, she performed two recitals in Steinert Hall, followed by

two more in March; after a summer in Paris, she resumed the season in October, and twice played the Tchaikovsky B-flat minor Concerto with the Philharmonic Society of New York, performed a solo program at the Playhouse in Chicago (a series also featuring that year Josef Hofmann, Pablo Casals, Jascha Heifetz, Sergei Rakhmaninov, and E. Robert Schmitz), and finished the year in New York on the League of Composers' first lecture recital, Olin Downes providing the lecture.

The 1924-25 season proceeded similarly, only with the additional responsibility of a five-year contract signed in January, 1925, to record on Welte piano rolls for the De Luxe Reproducing Roll Corporation. (On her contract Robinson pencilled "I made 10 records a year."[18]) In Oregon that spring she performed and conducted master classes and in the summer taught and performed as part of the faculty of Our Lady of the Lake College in San Antonio, Texas.

Critics from coast to coast acclaimed the energetic young Midwesterner with nearly uniform favor, and her agents delightedly quoted the most prominent. Often repeated were Felix Borowski's words after a Chicago recital when that respected critic fairly gushed:

> It is not saying too much in praise of her accomplishments as an interpreter of Chopin's music to declare that music has not been more convincingly set forth since Paderewski ravished the ear with it in a concert given last season at Orchestra Hall.[19]

Florence Ffrench, writing in *Musical Leader*, found equally glowing words:

> Carol Robinson created a veritable sensation by her magnificent playing. The young pianist, a long-time pupil and assistant to Mrs. Fannie Bloomfield Zeisler, gave an electrifying performance and aroused tremendous interest. Her interpretative charm, crystalline technic, admirable poise and remarkable control of dynamics all mark her as one of the most finished young artists of America. She belongs to the virtuoso class.[20]

"Miss Robinson," agreed the critic of the *Chicago Evening American*, "sings better with her fingers than many singers with their throats."[21]

After a New York debut at the Comedy Theatre in 1916, Richard Aldrich showed more reserve if no less enthusiasm:

Miss Robinson has a crisp and fluent technique and plays
with considerable taste, and with intelligent appreciation of
values. At a first hearing she gave the impression that her
best work is done in smaller numbers. . . Larger questions
may well be left for a second hearing—and her playing
yesterday [November 20, 1916] made it seem that a second
hearing would be worth while.[22]

And across the continent the critic for the *Los Angeles Times* joined in the
chorus of critical acclaim:

The enthusiastic demonstration received by Miss Carol
Robinson amounted to a triumph for this brilliant young
artist. Miss Robinson played the Bach-Liszt G-minor
fantasie and fugue like a master.[23]

Approving evaluations show up repeatedly in the Carol Robinson
Collection's news clippings and publicity brochures, several dramatically
illustrated with a reproduction of Joseph Stella's silverpoint drawing of
Carol. These establish beyond a doubt her position as a gifted, admired,
and even a first-rate pianist, at a time when women concert pianists
numbered very few.

At least as important as setting a course for others to follow were
Robinson's own distinctive contributions to American life. Among these
contributions there is first the question of where she made music.
Robinson had her share of evenings in the premier halls of the country,
Boston's Steinert, Chicago's Kimball, and New York's Aeolian, and
appearances with the major orchestras of each of these cities. However,
often sponsored by music clubs (the Fortnightly, the Amateur, the
Women's Century, the Zerelda Reading Club), Carol Robinson gave
dozens of performances outside these major centers: Muncie, Indiana;
Houghton, Michigan; Janesville, Wisconsin; Davenport, Iowa; Lawrence,
Kansas; Albany, New York; Peoria, Illinois; Medford, Oregon. In
homes, in schools, in colleges, and in churches, in the states of New
York, Massachusetts, Illinois, Indiana, Kansas, Missouri, Texas, Oregon,
and Washington, Carol Robinson brought music into the lives of
Americans.

On the one hand, the varied geography of her concert life shows
the degree to which Americans across the continent heard significant
contemporary music in the early decades of the twentieth century. At the
same time her frequent sponsors—various kinds of ladies' clubs—seem to
be the proverbial tip of a still inadequately recognized iceberg: the function of women's organizations in fostering America's cultural life. Only

recently have studies begun to acknowledge the part played by American women who, through club, school and church organizations, nurtured the spiritual life of the nation.[24] Undoubtedly, Carol first came to appreciate this network through her mother, a leader in founding Springfield's music club. While Carol could be impatient with women's "busy work," she valued their educational activities highly.

Robinson's audiences, both men and women, made up in enthusiasm what they often lacked in size; the *Daily Journal* reporter in Lawrence, Kansas, commented, "The fact that a group of 100 or slightly more could bring the artist out for three encores shows something of the program's success."[25] By mapping Robinson's performances, we begin to see the degree to which music of high quality permeated American life during the years documented by her programs, from 1914 until 1930. Americans across the land appeared encouragingly open-minded about music, especially in view of another aspect of her playing: her repertory.

Critics called the music Carol preferred "the ultramoderns." She selected more than one half of her extensive performance repertory from men and women active in composition. From Alaleona (Domenico) to Whitfield (Kathryn), with stops along the way for composers as diverse as Béla Bartók, Frank Bridge, Ulysses Kay, Christian Sinding, Alexander Steinert, Igor Stravinsky, and many others besides, Robinson gave music of her contemporaries a hearing. Although some of them admittedly kept Romantic musical traditions alive, such as Enrique Granados and Sergei Bortkiewicz, others, like Henry Cowell, led the avant garde. With many, including Cowell, she was personal friends; to all, she devoted her considerable intelligence and musicianship to such convincing interpretations of their works that one critic exclaimed: "Miss Robinson caused many to rise up and call modern music blessed!"[26] Audience members too expressed appreciative surprise for her devotion to contemporary music. After hearing her at Princeton in 1929, one layman wrote that the delight of hearing ultramodern music played in such a beautiful and intelligible fashion was a revelation.[27]

Robinson's programs show that she rarely played any program without a "modern group." And, in a practice highly unusual for the period, she devoted entire recitals to her contemporaries. Elizabeth Delza believes Carol Robinson in fact to be the first pianist to devote whole programs to twentieth-century music. In 1923 Robinson gave an all-modern recital of music and dance with the Frenchman, Henri (see Program 1a-c.) In 1929, appearing in New York at John Wanamaker's Belmaison Music Room, Carol gave the only recital of this series to be called "A Program of Modern Music." The repertoire for that occasion ("Afternoon Musicales with the Bechstein Pianoforte"), represents not only a devotion to contemporary music but also the kind of thoughtful planning for which critics lauded her. Usually arranging the music either chronologically or geographically, Robinson here chose the latter, having first a French, secondly a Russian, and finally an outside-the-European-mainstream group.[28] (The program is reproduced as Program 2a-b.) Characteristically during these years, she ended with Manuel de Falla's *Andaluza* and *Ritual Fire Dance*, two of her great favorites for curtain closers.

She often talked with audiences about the music in a way described as "quite marvelous," discussing the new rhythmic practices of Stravinsky and Bartók, explaining Schoenberg's harmonic ideas, and always illustrating with her incredible command of musical styles. From Illinois to Texas she demonstrated possibilities in exploring the piano's sonority with performances of Cowell's *Aeolian Harp*, a work the composer often called his "first piano string piece."[29] Performed by stroking, plucking and otherwise directly sounding the piano's strings, *Aeolian Harp*, probably written in 1923, created excitement virtually everywhere Carol performed it during her tour of 1926.

In such fashion Robinson frequently gave Americans their first taste of composers who later would become enshrined in history. In Boston, she gave the first performance music lovers in that city had ever heard of Georges Auric's *Sonatine*, then just two years old; of Darius Milhaud's *Sumaré*; and of Francis Poulenc's *Promenades*.[30] Her visits to Paris enriched her keyboard repertory not only with music of *Les Six* but also with that of outsiders active in the French capital. Thus, in Portland, Oregon, in 1926 Robinson appeared in the Second Referendum Concert of the Pro-Musica, playing works by George Antheil, Bohuslav Martinů, and Igor Stravinsky (a program discussed further in Part II).

Program 1a. A Dance Recital of Modern Music by Henri and Carol Robinson

A DANCE RECITAL OF MODERN MUSIC

BY

HENRI

AND CAROL ROBINSON PIANIST

MONDAY EVENING APRIL 23RD AT 9 O'CLOCK
THE ANDERSON GALLERIES AUDITORIUM
PARK AVENUE AND 59TH STREET
NEW YORK

FOURTH RECITAL OF SEASON

Program 1b. A Dance Recital of Modern Music, cont.

PROGRAMME

IMPRESSIONS OF A VOYAGE THROUGH CRIMEA	MOUSSORGSKY
SPACE	
ETUDE OPUS 2 NO. 1	SCRIABIN
TIME	
PROMENADE THROUGH A PICTURE GALLERY	MOUSSORGSKY
FROM "TABLEAU D'UN EXPOSITION"	
ARABESQUE NO. 2	DEBUSSY
IT IS A BIRD FLYING	

HENRI

POEME OPUS 31 NO. 2	SCRIABIN
MOUVEMENTS PERPETUELS	POULENC
PIECE BREVE NO. 7	HONEGGER

CAROL ROBINSON

PAVANNE FOR THE DEATH OF A ROYAL CHILD	RAVEL
SUMARE	MILHAUD
FROM "SANDADES DO BRAZIL"	
THE BURIED CATHEDRAL	DEBUSSY
CAPRICE	PROKOFIEFF
THAT GRAND OLD HYMNAL ANTI-CLIMAX	

HENRI

DANSE EXOTIQUE	STEINERT
ONDINE	RAVEL
DANSE	DE FALLA
FROM "ELAMOR BRUJO"	

CAROL ROBINSON

THREE LITTLE FUNERAL MARCHES	BERNERS
(A) FOR A MAN OF STATE	
(B) FOR A CANARY BIRD	
(C) FOR A RICH AUNT	
DANSE NEGRE	SCOTT
THE BLACK CAT IN THE SUMMERTIME	
TANGO-CHANT	HENRI

HENRI

MASON AND HAMLIN PIANO USED

Program 1c. A Dance Recital of Modern Music, cont.

COMMENTS

The pseudo — Greek dance dead and buried; for our joy Henri's dancing asserts itself, unique, vital and inevitable in the adventure through untrodden paths.

Joseph Stella

Henri commence ou les autres danseurs finissent.

Georgette Leblanc

The most beautiful and important dancing I have seen.

Emanuel Carnavali

A beginning of the abstract in dancing which should clear up for the public mind the confusion evidently still existing as to the representative antics of an Isadora Duncan.

Margaret Anderson
PUBLISHER OF *THE LITTLE REVIEW*

Henri will carry the modern word in art with distinction wherever he penetrates with his dances.

William Carlos Williams

*Single subscription to this recital is three dollars
Subscriptions should be made payable to
Mollie Higgins Smith at the
Anderson Galleries*

AFTERNOON MUSICALES

WITH THE

BECHSTEIN
PIANOFORTE

*

MONDAY, MAY 20th TO FRIDAY, MAY 24th, 1929
AT THREE O'CLOCK

*

BELMAISON MUSIC ROOM

FIFTH GALLERY · NEW BUILDING

JOHN WANAMAKER NEW YORK

Program 2b. Afternoon musicales with the Bechstein Pianoforte

THURSDAY, MAY 23

CAROL ROBINSON, *Pianist*

Program of Modern Music

I

Delphic Dancers
Valse "la plus que lente . . . " } · · · · **Debussy**
Ondine · · · · · · · · · · · **Ravel**
Promenades:
      En Pied
      En Cheval } · · · · · **Poulenc**
      En Diligence
Bourree Fantasque · · · · · · · **Chabrier**

II

Poeme Op. 31, No. 2 · · · · · · · **Scriabin**
Vision Fugitive · · · · · · · · **Prokofieff**
Two Etudes:
      F Sharp Minor }
      C Sharp Minor } · · · · · **Bortkiewicz**
Chez Petrouchka · · · · · · · **Stravinsky**

III

Waltz · · · · · · · · · · · **Beecher**
Clog Dance · · · · · · · · · **Hanson**
Par T. S. F. · · · · · · · · · **Martinu**
Elegie · · · · · · · · · · · **Bartok**
Andaluza
Danse Rituelle du Feu } · · · · · **De Falla**

In 1993, after almost a century of "new music," one can rather glibly cite Carol Robinson's pioneering efforts without her importance truly registering. Yet performers routinely encountered serious difficulties in bringing contemporary music before the public. Examining Edgard Varèse's founding of an organization for new music in America, Allen Lott quotes the composer's amazement "that nobody knew anything about modern music."[31] After Eva Gautier's recital in Aeolian Hall, the *Little Review* editor noted: "Gautier has introduced more than seven hundred songs, by new or unknown composers to the public. We hope there is a reward for that kind of energy somewhere: it is not in the box-office."[32] Marion Bauer and Claire R. Reis, whose involvement with the League of Composers put them squarely in a position to see how difficult was "the problem of finding artists who were interested in interpreting modern works,"[33] found that those who dared to tackle the music of contemporaries were rare.

Carol Robinson was one of the few who dared. One of her promotional pamphlets of these years in dramatic black and white features Carol in a photograph by Mortimer Offner. The text reads in part:

> If you love music and are alive to the age in which we are living, you must be interested in the music of this age. You will want to hear, and study, and develop an appreciation for...the music that has been written for you—not for a previous generation.
>
> It is possible to hear the best of modern music, at least twice a year in New York in the Concerts of the two organizations devoted to the advancement of modern composers: the International Composers' Guild and the League of Composers. But what about the splendid audience outside of New York?[34]

The pamphlet (reproduced as Program 3) goes on to offer the opportunity to hear the best of modern music without having to go to New York, through the lectures, recitals, discussions, and master classes of Carol Robinson.

Program 3a.   Modern Music: Carol Robinson

Program 3b. Modern Music: Carol Robinson

HOW DO YOU GET YOUR CONTACT WITH MODERN MUSIC

IF YOU LOVE MUSIC AND ARE ALIVE TO THE AGE IN WHICH WE ARE LIVING, YOU MUST BE INTERESTED IN THE MUSIC OF THIS AGE. YOU WILL WANT TO HEAR, AND STUDY, AND DEVELOP AN APPRECIATION FOR THE TEMPERAMENT, A DIFFERENT AUDITORY SYSTEM, THE MUSIC THAT HAS BEEN WRITTEN FOR YOU . . . NOT FOR A PREVIOUS GENERATION, WITH A DIFFERENT NEW MUSIC IS A FORCE THAT IS SHAPING OUR LIVES TODAY.

IT IS POSSIBLE TO HEAR THE BEST OF MODERN MUSIC, AT LEAST TWICE A YEAR IN NEW YORK, IN THE CONCERTS OF THE TWO ORGANIZATIONS DEVOTED TO THE ADVANCEMENT OF MODERN COMPOSERS: THE INTERNATIONAL COMPOSERS GUILD AND THE LEAGUE OF COMPOSERS. BUT WHAT ABOUT THE SPLENDID AUDIENCE OUTSIDE OF NEW YORK?

MODERN ART IN ALL ITS FORMS HAS COME INTO ITS OWN VIBRANTLY AND DYNAMICALLY. ALL SCHOOLS, COLLEGES, UNIVERSITIES, AND OTHER EDUCATIONAL GROUPS SHOULD BE INTERESTED IN PRESENTING TO THE YOUTH OF TODAY . . . THE ART OF TODAY. THE LITTLE THEATRE, THAT STRONG FORCE FOR EDUCATION, CAN DO AS MUCH FOR THE PROMOTION OF MODERN MUSIC AS IT HAS DONE FOR THE THEATRE. WE WANT TO AFFILIATE WITH YOU . . EDUCATION AND LITTLE THEATRE! OUR WORK IS PARALLEL TO YOURS.

CAROL ROBINSON
126 EAST TWENTY-EIGHTH STREET
NEW YORK

DIRECTION - - - - - R. NEWMAN

RECITALS OF WORK
BY

STRAVINSKY	GRIFFES
ANTHEIL	HANSON
HONNEGER	STEINERT
CASELLA	DE FALLA
GOOSENS	COWELL
MARTINU	MILHAUD
MESENS	SATIE
WHITHORNE	MALIPIERO
SCHOENBERG	AURIC
POULENC	SZYMANOWSKY
RUDYHAR	PROKOFIEFF
SCRIABIN	

PROGRAMS

WE ARE PREPARED TO GIVE RECITALS OF THE WORK OF THE FOREMOST COMPOSERS, OF EUROPE AND OF AMERICA. THE GREATEST ACTIVITY AMONG THE YOUNGER MEN HAS BEEN IN COMPOSITIONS FOR THE PIANO. . . . A LARGER CONTACT WITH MODERN MUSIC CAN THEREFORE BE HAD THROUGH PIANO MUSIC. WE WILL ARRANGE REQUEST PROGRAMS TO SUPPLEMENT REGULAR COURSES; WE WILL ARRANGE GALA PROGRAMS FOR SPECIAL FETE DAYS, SPRING FESTIVALS, ETC. . . . WE ARE PREPARED TO COVER THE COMPLETE FIELD OF PIANO-MUSIC, IN AN EDUCATIONAL AS WELL AS AN ARTISTIC MANNER, FROM SCRIABINE TO THE MOST STRIDENT OF THE YOUNG COMPOSERS: GEORGE ANTHEIL, THE YOUNG AMERICAN, COMPOSER OF THE "BALLET MECANIQUE."

DISCUSSION

CAROL ROBINSON HAS A THOROUGH FOUNDATION IN THE MUSIC OF THE PAST AND IS PREPARED TO DISCUSS MUSIC IN ALL ITS FORMS. SHE WILL DEMONSTRATE THE NEW MECHANICS OF MUSIC IN CONTRAST WITH THE OLDER METHODS. QUESTIONS WILL BE INVITED . . . . COMPOSITION ENCOURAGED. SPECIAL CLASSES CAN BE ARRANGED ON TOUR, OR PUPILS INTERESTED IN EXTENSION WORK MAY JOIN THE NEW YORK CLASSES, AT A NOT UNREASONABLE FEE.

The handful of musicians who like Carol endeavored to bring contemporary music to the "splendid audience" outside of New York sometimes found remarkable enthusiasm. The daughter of E. Robert Schmitz, speaking of the Pro-Musica Chapters her father established across America, recalled that

> the reception in the most unlikely places was excellent. This was something that always astonished Father. In places that we, as European snobs, felt would never have good reactions, you could find people who suddenly fall totally in love with Poulenc! It was a very strange phenomenon in the twenties. It was a sort of crazy and wide-open American scene.[35]

Although Carol Robinson performed and lectured extensively on her own, she also joined other prominent groups in the realm of modern music. Her enthusiasm for Skryabin led her not only to program the Russian's music with frequency but also to join a Skryabin Club in New York, where she became friends with Skryabin's biographer Faubion Bowers. In addition to appearing in Oregon with the Pro-Musica and in New York with the League of Composers, she twice performed with the International Composers Guild, once in Ildebrando Pizzetti's *Trio for Violin, Piano, and Cello*, and a second time in Paul Hindemith's *Der Damon* (in which she played celesta).[36]

Through the nature of her performance activites, Carol Robinson emerges as an individual committed to giving the living composer the opportunity to experiment. Whether in an ensemble or alone, in lecture-recitals or in interviews, she lived her commitment with intensity and with devotion, convincingly bringing forth music for which she helped to build an audience. While the role of such organizations as the International Composers' Guild and the League of Composers, to both of which Carol contributed, undoubtedly helped to change public, or at least New York, attitudes, Carol Robinson, playing alone, lecturing individually, and teaching new music, initiated many citizens across America into the music of the twentieth century.

NOTES

1.   *Greenville Advocate*, 27 January 1898, clipping in the family papers of Phoebe Sells, Robinson's niece. Mrs. Sells has contrib-

uted pictures, programs, and her own genealogical research on the Robinson family to benefit the present study.

2.   LS Phoebe Sells, 6 March 1989, including W. E. Robinson's obituary clipped from the *Poultry Item*, March 1936.

3.   LS Eleanor Robinson, 23 January 1989. Carol's nephew David Robinson and his wife Eleanor have liberally aided this study with personal materials, family records, programs and pictures in their possession.

4.   *Illinois State Journal*, ? August 1939, pp. 3-4, clipping in the family papers of Phoebe Sells.

5.   Clipping included in LS Phoebe Sells, 6 March 1989.

6.   *The News Bulletin of the LAA* 16/3 (1958): 6.

7.   *The National Cyclopedia of American Biography*, 1917 ed., 14: 193.

8.   Ibid.

9.   *The News Bulletin of the LAA* 16/3 (1958): 6. Mrs. Sells recalls that Carol thus met Albert Einstein, with whom she played violin and piano duets.

10.   *The Dictionary of American Biography*, Authors edition, 20: 648.

11.   *News Bulletin of the LAA* 16/3 (1958): 6.

12.   Margaret Anderson, *My Thirty Years' War* (New York: Covici, Friede Publishers, 1930), p. 16. For an account of Zeisler's teaching methods, see Theodora Troendle, "How Fannie Bloomfield Zeisler Taught," *Etude* 47 (1929): 799-800.

13.   Kindly quoted by Diana Hallman from *Fannie Bloomfield Zeisler, An Appreciation* (Chicago: 1927), p. 7, in letter to the author, 20 July 1988. In these years, according to Hjordis Halvorson of Chicago's Newberry Library, the *Chicago City Directory* for 1910 lists Carol Robinson, "music teacher," as maintaining a studio on Michigan Avenue in Chicago and living at 5729 Calumet, not far from the Zeislers.

14. *News Bulletin of the LAA* 16/3 (1958): 6.

15. Herman DeVries, "Carol Robinson in Adolf Weidig Program," clipping in GU MS 300, Box 4, Folder Chicago: Orchestra Hall.

16. Ibid.

17. Telephone interview with David Robinson, 7 November 1988.

18. "Agreement with De Luxe Reproducing Corporation," GU MS 300, Box 1, Folder 2. A list of the piano rolls Robinson made appears in Appendix C.

19. Promotional pamphlet "Carol Robinson, Distinguished American Pianist," Management Loro Gooch, Auditorium Building, Chicago, GU MS 300, Box 1, Folder 1.

20. Ibid.

21. Flyer of press comments, 21 November 1916, GU MS 300, Box 1, Folder 1.

22. *The New York Times*, 21 November 1916, p. 9.

23. Clipping in GU MS 300, Box 1, Folder 10.

24. See, for example, Linda Whitesitt, "The Role of Women's Music Clubs in Shaping American Concert Life, 1870-1930," paper presented before the American Musicological Society, Baltimore, Maryland, November 1988, and Anne Firor Scott, *Making the Invisible Woman Visible* (Urbana and Chicago: University of Illinois Press, 1984).

25. "Miss Robinson's Recital Pleases," *Daily Journal*, 18 March 1926, clipping in GU MS 300, Box 1, Folder 10.

26. Promotional pamphlet "Carol Robinson, Pianist," Management Richard Newman, Steinert Hall, Boston, GU MS 300, Box 1, Folder 1. The pamphlet attributes the quote to the *Chicago Herald Examiner* after a program of 26 October 1924.

27. LS Alexander Russell, 10 May 1929, GU MS 300, Box 1, Folder 2.

28.   23 May 1929, GU MS 300, Box 4, Folder New York: Belmaison Music Room.

29.   William Lichtenwanger, *The Music of Henry Cowell, A Descriptive Catalogue*, I.S.A.M. monographs, no. 23 (Brooklyn, New York: Institute for Studies in American Music, 1986), p. 94.

30.   According to Robinson's program, 4 March 1924, in GU MS 300, Box 4, Folder Boston: Steinert Hall.

31.   R. Allen Lott, "'New Music for New Ears': The International Composers' Guild," *Journal of the American Musicological Society* 36 (1983): 267.

32.   *The Little Review*, Autumn-Winter 1923-24, p. 38.

33.   Marion Bauer and Claire R. Reis, "Twenty-five Years with the League of Composers," *Musical Quarterly* 34 (1948): 5.

34.   Promotional pamphlet "Modern Music Carol Robinson," Management Richard Newman, GU MS 300, Box 1, Folder 1.

35.   Quoted in Vivian Perlis, *Two Men for Modern Music. E. Robert Schmitz and Herman Langinger*, I.S.A.M. monographs, no. 9 (Brooklyn, N.Y.: Institute for Studies of American Music, 1978), p. 11.

36.   Robinson's name is omitted from the Guild's performer lists in the article "'New Music'" for JAMS; however, the Guild's printed programs (November 28, 1926 and January 30, 1927) and subsequent press reports show that Robinson performed on both occasions.

CHAPTER 2

CAROL ROBINSON, TEACHER

As effective as her playing seems to have been, it is very likely in her teaching that Carol Robinson had the greatest influence. She herself believed that teaching was an art. The conventional notion that if you can't do, you teach, she dismissed as ridiculous.

A teacher's influence eludes precise measure, although the superficial evidence is easily documented. She attracted many fine students, including those of distinguished families, such as Gloria Caruso, daughter of Enrico and Dorothy Caruso; and Iovanna Wright, daughter of Frank Lloyd and Olgivanna Wright. Among her students who established notable musical careers were Ruth Bradley, pianist and composer who died tragically and unexpectedly in 1963,[1] and Julie Steinberg, today on the Mills College faculty and an outstanding interpreter of twentieth-century music. She also held numerous teaching positions: at the Convent of St. Francis, Oldenburg, Indiana, (summers, 1926, 1927); at Our Lady of the Lake College, San Antonio, Texas, (summers, 1925, 1926); at New York University (summer, 1927); as Director of the Music Department, Rosemont College, Rosemont, Pennsylvania, (1933-1939); as teacher of harmony and piano at the Association for Music and Art on Cape Cod, Centerville, Massachusetts (summer, 1940); as member of the Dalcroze School Faculty, New York, (1952-1959); and at Smith College (1953-54). And she presented dozens of recitals at schools and colleges around the United States (see Appendix A). Through all these years Robinson maintained a private studio in her Manhattan apartment at 405 East 54th Street.

Yet the real substance of teaching—developing the individual's potential, illuminating willing minds, guiding the process of self discovery—these things do not distill into lines on a *curriculum vitae*. That Carol Robinson remains alive in the minds of so many whom she touched offers the best evidence of her influence. "Not a day goes by that I do not think of what she taught me," several maintain. Others recount her ability to communicate the matters of music: the touch to achieve a "singing tone" (demonstrated with just the right pressure on the student's shoulder), the possible range of tempos (Richter plays it at this tempo, marked in the student's score), and the all-important factor, the musical IDEA (with frequent cautions about the pianist "who is meticulous in playing every note on the page with clarity, but who never succeeds in projecting a musical idea with simplicity and beauty"[2]).

Uniformly, her students recall the introduction Robinson gave to all kinds of music, eliciting as much sympathy for the living composer as for the past masters of keyboard literature. Her own lists of recommended music literature found among her papers and her teaching scores in the University of Georgia School of Music's reference library bear out these reports, for Bartók, Bloch, Alfred Casella, Debussy, Glière, Ted Kassern (*Teen-Age Concerto*), Colin McPhee, and Stravinsky take place alongside Bach, Beethoven, and Chopin in the training of Carol's students. ("I was raised on Bartók," one recalls, "and studied the *Mikrokosmos* from the age of 8." Another recounts being sent home as a child with a page of Ives's difficult *Concord Sonata* to "see what you can do.")

Carol Robinson did not teach just music; in the words of one of her students, she taught the whole person. From directing the movement of a pupil's head and neck to the role of the torso in performance, Robinson believed in the total physical involvement of the pianist. Her nephew recalls that she was writing a book for pianists on "The Left Foot."[3] Her keen appreciation for the physical dimensions of musical performance shows in her involvement with dancers. In "A Dance Recital of Modern Music by Henri" (see Program 1), Carol played mostly French and Russian works to improvisations by the Frenchman who was enthralling the art world.[4] During the 'thirties and 'forties she worked closely with Elizabeth Delza (the dancer who is also known as Mrs. Gorham Munson). Not surprisingly, Robinson eventually appeared on the faculty of the Dalcroze School (1952-59), where pupils learn music through movement from an early age, but her own students describe her teaching as "beyond Dalcroze."

It was not only her teaching philosophies that distinguished Carol Robinson; it was that she personified her own high ideals. People today use words such as "incredible," "extraordinary," "an inspiration," "a great presence" in an effort to communicate what she was like. With her friends fun-loving, easy, gracious, and giving, telling lively stories in her bell-like voice, with herself she sought depths of strength that few ever tap. This is nowhere more evident than in the frequently told incidents of her last years when, in intense pain, she nevertheless presented a composed countenance to students and friends alike. Her letters describe "fairly hideous nights" and confide that often after a lesson, she would collapse in an agony unsuspected by the student.[5] For a person of more than eighty years of age to achieve such control implies a lifetime of self discipline.

By all accounts, Carol Robinson's concentration on her own musicianship was a consuming one, providing far better by example than by command the almost magical alignment of self awareness at every level. Her rich inner life clearly manifested itself to those who knew her, touching those who met her only once as well as those closest to her. A pioneer in championing the music of "the moderns," Carol Robinson represented for many a model for living. As one of her students said fervently, "I consider her a pioneer in personhood."

NOTES

1. On Ruth Bradley, see *The News Bulletin of the LAA* 17/31 (1959): 12-13 and 21/35 (1964): 18.

2. Teaching or Lecture Notes, GU MS 300, Box 1, Folder 3. Jean Réti-Forbes had planned for Robinson's papers to belong to a Great Teachers' Collection in the Hargrett Library.

3. Telephone interview with David Robinson, 7 November 1988. No manuscript has, however, surfaced.

4. Monday, 23 April (no year given; probably 1923), GU MS 300, Box 4, Folder: New York, Anderson Galleries. This program includes tributes to Henri (pronounced with a long i) from Margaret Anderson, Joseph Stella, Georgette Leblanc, Emanuel Carnevali, and William Carlos Williams. For a lengthier tribute by Carnevali, see "Dancing as an Art: To Henri," *The Little Review*, June 1919, pp. 26-28.

5. Carol apparently suffered from post herpetic neuralgia, an extremely painful and disabling condition (for some understanding of which I am indebted to Athens neurologist Dr. Van Morris). She mentions her suffering in several letters to Jean Réti-Forbes: LS 12 April 1972; and LS 21 September (no year), GU MS 912, General Correspondence, Box "Ro-She."

CHAPTER 3

CAROL ROBINSON, COMPOSER

Carol Robinson composed from her earliest years in Fannie Bloomfield Zeisler's studio until she was an old woman. Although not always remarkable for their intrinsic value, Robinson's compositions show her personal responses to various aspects of twentieth-century experience. They also round out the compelling example of her life as a complete musician, who performed, taught, composed, and read widely.

Robinson had studied composition in Chicago, with Adolf Weidig, Thorwald Otterstroem, and Carl Beecher.[1] The most prominent seems to have been Weidig, a well-respected pedagogue who also taught Carol's friend Marie Pierik (later a Gregorian chant enthusiast) and Ruth Crawford (who distinquished herself as an innovative and gifted composer). Weidig (1867-1931), a student of Ludwig Spohr and of "the great Dr. [Hugo] Riemann," had come to Chicago at the end of the nineteenth century where he joined the orchestra and eventually became associate director of the American Conservatory. When Robinson made her performance debut with the Chicago Symphony in 1921, Weidig preceded her on the program, conducting his own *Three Episodes*, Op. 38. His Tristan-like composition elicited the following comment from critic Ruth Miller: "He is among the last of the classically faithful, and we know that he will never desert the musical standard of yesterday."[2]

Robinson's earliest works, which show up with some frequency on her piano recitals, have all the earmarks of the late romantic style that Weidig perpetuated. As an example, a prelude composed in 1919 and dedicated to Fannie Bloomfield Zeisler has a key signature of E-flat minor, frequent chromatic passing tones, and an abundance of rich chords, some altered, some borrowed, some with added seventh, ninth, and eleventh scale degrees. The recurring theme, its lyricism and arpeggiated accompaniment strongly reminiscent of Chopin, takes an intensely chromatic route on its way from the tonic to the subdominant, and eventually to the more tonally distant regions of E minor and E major (see Appendix B, p. 214).

More than one of these early works drew favorable contemporary comments. *Two Intermezzi* prompted Mrs. Zeisler to remark: "The second is much prettier than the first. I wish this had been written before Debussy's time."[3] Her preludes gained an even warmer reception. "When it came to her own three preludes," reported the *Journal of*

Commerce after her performance November 4, 1920, "the second, with its whimsical ending, had to be played twice, and so insistent was the applause that its young composer might have given it a third hearing."[4] That this style enjoyed wide acceptance among American music circles may be inferred from Welte's marketing decision to have Carol Robinson record her *Prelude* in F-sharp minor[5] and from the award she received from the National Federation of Music Clubs for *Silence of Amor*.[6] This art song and its companion, *Shadowy Woodlands*, share the same effulgent harmonizations found in the piano music from these years. The song texts also share the same poet, Fiona Macleod, perhaps their most remarkable trait.

Example 1, *Shadowy Woodlands*, mm. 1-6.

One of the strangest literary figures of the turn of the century, Fiona Macleod's real identity became known only at the death of its owner, William Sharp (1855-1905), a prolific author of biographies, short stories, novels, and art and literary criticism. For reasons still something of a mystery, Sharp preferred to bring forth his poetic visions of life in the Celtic highlands under a carefully guarded, female, pseudonym. Although the revelation of the literary hoax perpetrated on an unsuspecting public eventually cast Sharp's literary reputation into a steady decline, the prose poems of Fiona Macleod initially captivated quite a number of Americans. Among these appears the music critic Lawrence Gilman, who corresponded with Fiona Macleod, responding warmly to a letter from "her." Gilman first acknowledged "The deep impressions which your own work has made upon me" and then observed, "You would be surprised, I think, to know how the Celtic impulse is seizing the imaginations of some of the younger and more warmly-tempered of American composers."[7] Among these warmly-tempered Americans figured Edward MacDowell, who also corresponded with Fiona Macleod;[8] Henry Cowell, whose Celtic inspirations range from *The Banshee* to Irish jigs; and Carol Robinson.

If Robinson's musical interpretations of Macleod's texts embody nineteenth-century sweetness, they also reveal what seems to have appealed to many about Fiona Macleod's poetry: "the pain and passion of a Gaelic chant." Robinson created a declamatory line for the voice that preserved the rhythm of these prose-poems in flexible, changing meters. She also wisely avoided pianistic display in the keyboard part, which she kept subdued with block chords that quietly support the voice, *una corde* pedal markings, and dynamic levels of *piano* and *pianissimo*.

Two settings from the poetry of Emily Dickinson, *I'll Tell You How the Sun Rose* and *The Moon Was But a Chin of Gold*, and one each of Elinor Wylie and Hilda Doolittle show Robinson celebrating the literary creativity of "real" women, all Americans. Emily Dickinson's nearly 900 poems, found in manuscript at her death in 1886, only gradually appeared in print in the course of the twentieth century, and Robinson was among the first to give them musical settings. For the verse "I'll tell you how the sun rose," Robinson created quite a spritely musical interpretation. The music moves *Allegretto* in rapid sixteenth notes, flowing easily from 5/8 meter into 10/8, then into 3/4 and 7/8 before ending in 6/8. The piano plays what is essentially a two-voice counterpoint to the voice line and from time to time paints the vocalist's text (ascending intervals to a high chord at the words "That must have been the sun"; a shift into minor mode at "purple stile"; a whole-tone melody at "little yellow boys and girls"). The overall harmonic motion, from E major into G major and

back around to E, emphasizes the kinds of alternative tonal relationships
being explored in the post-Romantic world.

In her manuscript, Robinson underlined the poems' words "sun"
and "moon" in each song, and she seems to explore their contrast
musically: "I'll tell you how the sun rose" is in E major and *Allegretto*;
"The moon was but a chin of gold" is in A minor and *Andantino*. "The
moon" is further marked *legatissimo, sempre senza pedale*. This dreamy
little piece of twenty measures, a miniature like the poem it sets, forms
a delicate duet between the voice and the pianist, who often plays but a
single line (Example 2).

Example 2, *The moon was but a chin of gold*, mm. 1-4.

The music reflects the intimacy between moon and poet and perhaps depicts the isolation of the eccentric spinster Dickinson herself. Piano and voice depend on one another throughout—for harmonic definition, for contrapuntal interest, for completion of rhythmic thoughts. Robinson marked the meter here simply "8"—meaning varying groups of eighth notes that change with each measure. While the voice line is entirely diatonic (suggesting the "pure" poet always dressed in white), the piano has one brief foray into chromaticism, heightening the sensuality of the words "Her lips of amber never part."

Although Robinson could not have known Emily Dickinson, she may well have been friends or at least acquaintances with the American poets Elinor Hoyt Wylie (1885-1928) and H.D., as Hilda Doolittle (1886-1961) was known. The beautiful and witty Elinor Hoyt scandalized American society by leaving her husband and young son for Washington lawyer Horace Wylie in 1910. Living for a time in London and then in Augusta, Georgia, Elinor eventually separated from her lawyer and came to New York in the early 1920s, as did Robinson. Marrying William Rose Benét in 1923, Elinor enthralled New York literary circles with her elegance and conversation before her untimely death. A point of contact between Elinor Wylie and Robinson may have been the literary critic A.R. Orage, editor of *The New Age* and effective propagandist for the intriguing Gurdjieff. Both Wylie and Robinson sought out Orage in New York for critiques of their literary efforts. Robinson's family still owns a letter from the critic, dated December 20, 1927, encouraging the pianist in her writing. And, in what seems to be the same year, Louise Welch, a friend of Robinson, a devotee of Wylie, and a follower of Orage and Gurdjieff, reported having encountered Elinor Wylie coming from Orage's apartment.[9] Mrs. Welch eventually learned that the poet too had requested direction for her writing from Orage. Certainly, both Wylie and Robinson shared the ambition to realize the self, a realization which in Wylie's case was often smothered beneath the decorative surface of her beauty.

In her setting of Wylie's *Velvet Shoes*, Robinson modified the overripe harmonic writing of her earliest works. Perhaps she was inspired by the text, a poetic evocation of myriad images for white. Robinson captured whiteness and its musical counterpart, silence, in quiet consonant chords marching quietly through the piano's score. Meanwhile, the voice moves mostly stepwise, in triplet and duplet eighths, to the piano's steady quarter-note tread (Example 3). The music manuscripts include a page on which the composer converted the spoken poetic rhythms of *Velvet Shoes* into musical ones in preparation for composing. The sketch suggests how she achieved so intimate a fusion of poetic and musical means in this song as well as in others.

Example 3, *Velvet Shoes*, mm. 1-4.

With the music she created for Hilda Doolittle's *Never More Will the Wind*, Robinson stripped her style of chromaticism and vastly simplified the piano writing by comparison with the Fiona Macleod settings. The voice, sounding almost free in its declamation, mourns hauntingly over the piano's plain triads, seldom flavored with even the seventh degree. The tiny, twelve-measure work recalls Richard Aldrich's somewhat patronizing comment on Robinson's playing that "she is best in smaller numbers," an observation that may hold for her composing more than her playing (Example 4).

Example 4, *Never More Will the Wind*, mm. 1-4.

The poet of *Never More Will the Wind*, the Imagist known as "H.D.," lived most of her life abroad. However, her brief engagement to Ezra Pound, a friend of Robinson, and her connections to Robinson's friends of *The Little Review* (about whom we will learn more in Chapter 4) may have brought Hilda Doolittle into personal contact with Carol Robinson. H.D.'s career revolved around her own search for personal identity as both a woman and an artist. In that search she wrote a great deal of poetry that reshaped classical myth to modern form as a means of achieving a sense of the spiritual and the timeless.[10] The words of *Never More Will the Wind*, for example, form part of a masque set in ancient Greece. Called *Hymen* (1921), the masque portrays women of all ages participating in the familiar ritual of a wedding. H.D.'s stage directions specify "deep, chanting music" and accompaniment of flute, harp, and woodwind. Young women sing the words of *Never More Will the Wind* to the bride, their playmate who will leave them forever for a new life.

Standing alone, in Carol Robinson's song, the words seem to mourn someone's death. As did many women who came of age in the 'twenties, Robinson never married. Perhaps H.D.'s poem articulated Robinson's own recognition that for women marriage often means death—at least in the sense of creativity and independence. However, Carol Robinson was no chauvinist on behalf of her sex. While presumably she chose H.D.'s poem because she found in its words some response to her own thoughts, her choice of women's poetry seems primarily motivated by her quest for achieved excellence, a quest that was gender free. A loyal friend to men and women alike, as we shall see, Robinson saw the person, not the sex, of an individual and genuinely rejoiced in the artistry and spiritual growth of others.

Although Carol Robinson presumably simplified her style in these songs partly because of her sensitivity to the poetry, other forces were also shaping her ideas. Far from the *Prelude* in E-flat minor and its chromatic harmony are the melodic exercises she composed for her pupils, featuring drones for the left hand and a melody for the right hand founded on a non-standard scale graced with an Oriental-sounding ornament.

Example 5, *Pedagogical Exercise No. 4.*

Although some remember that in later years Robinson took composition lessons with Edgard Varèse, the progressive Frenchman who moved to New York in 1915, this exercise and other works seem to owe little to Varèse's experimental style. The influence toward this new way of writing almost certainly lies elsewhere.

In 1924 Carol Robinson went to Boston to perform with the Boston Symphony. While there she heard a presentation by a remarkable man, Georgi Gurdjieff.[11] A native of Goumairi (until recently Leninaken), Gurdjieff had spent years searching for the meaning of life, a search that had led him from Armenia to the sands of the Sahara to the monasteries of Tibet. Urged west by the Bolshevik revolution, Gurdjieff settled just outside Paris at Fontainebleau-Avon, where he established his Institute for the Harmonious Development of Man. There to daily manual labor, sumptuous meals, dance-like temple exercises, and endless readings of Gurdjieff's manuscript "Beelzebub's Tales to his Grandson," pupils endeavored "to find the I," to balance man's centers of emotional, intellectual and physical activity. Some followers remained for years, even in Gurdjieff's absence. Some, like Katherine Mansfield, died there, having sought him out at the ends of their lives. Others—like the French acoustician, novelist, and composer Pierre Schaeffer (b. 1910), creator of musique concrète—gravitated there for communal living. People came to him from all over the world, although Gurdjieff found ways to discourage all but those willing and able to dedicate themselves fully to the "Work."

Gurdjieff and selected dancers came to America for the first time in 1924. Gorham Munson reports in The Awakening Twenties that

> People who had no use for the ideas of Gurdjieff excepted
> the dances from their censure; the dances, they said, were
> strange and wonderful. And indeed it was a unique and
> profound experience that they gave. There had never
> before been anything like them in America.[12]

In America, Gurdjieff singled out Carol Robinson.[13] So taken was she with his manner, his system of ideas, and his promise of a higher life that she travelled that summer to his Institute at Fontainebleau. There Robinson lived on the "Monks' Corridor" rather than the Ritz, the followers' name for the second floor with Gurdjieff's bedroom.[14] She found that music occupied an essential part of the spiritual exercises. Dictated by Gurdjieff, the music was notated and harmonized by others, most notably Thomas de Hartmann, a Russian composer who had followed Gurdjieff to Paris. Although the music was kept secret for a long time, Hartmann did bring forth an edition before his death.[15] The music bears many of the same features as Carol Robinson's piano exercises: persistent left-hand drones, a narrow melodic compass set in a non-conventional scale, and similar ornaments.

Carol Robinson became one of the leading performers of the Gurdjieff music and, by several accounts, the guru's special favorite. A few remember her relating how she would work all day at some physical task—such as digging a ditch that Gurdjieff was sure to have them fill in again the next day—only to come in and play the exercises until late in the night. Some people believe that Gurdjieff's emphasis on the rich inner life led Robinson to turn from the more glamourous public career of performing to the quieter one of teaching. Certainly, until Gurdjicff's death in 1949, she performed less and less with major Western orchestras and regularly with Gurdjieff groups in New York. Despite her own silence about this teacher (a vow most followers observe), those closest to her testify that Gurdjieff's teachings became central to her life, second only to music.

Because of Gurdjieff, Robinson met many gifted individuals with whom she collaborated. Among them were the literary critic Gorham Munson and his wife, the dancer Elizabeth Delza. On coming to New York from Russia, Delza established the Elizabeth Delza School of Dance on New York's Fifth Avenue in 1936. She taught modern dance forms, ancient sacred dances to modern poetry, and dances to contrapuntal music. Robinson frequently insisted that her piano pupils enroll in Delza's classes, where they learned to interpret the voices of Baroque fugues through separate head, arm, and leg movements. These pupils often studied with Robinson and Delza jointly until college age. Those who observed or participated in Delza's classes marvelled at how "she expanded the whole realm of music" for young people.[16] Delza shared with Carol an enthusiasm for the physical dimension of musical performance, for teaching, and for Gurdjieff. Together they gave recitals that included the secret Gurdjieff music and dances (although these remained unidentified on the printed programs; examples are *The Four Dances* from unpublished music in Program 4). Robinson composed a *Chorale Dance* for Delza that recalls the stately processionals of the Renaissance, its irregular phrasing and frequent meter changes achieving the same rhythmic flexibility evident in her vocal music (Example 6). If Delza's movements to the *Chorale Dance* recreated the sensuous character of the Renaissance dance, Robinson's minor mode and parallelisms perhaps reflect Gurdjieff's world, a world which bound her philosophically to Delza.

Program 4. Dance Recital Elizabeth Delza

FIRST CONCERT

July 18, 1940   8:30 P.M.

DANCE RECITAL

E L I Z A B E T H   D E L Z A

Carol Robinson and Ralph Lawton, Pianists

P R O G R A M

I
DANCES WITH OLD MUSIC

1. Sinfonia, Adagio and Andante [from Partita II]   Bach
2. Polonaise [from B minor Suite]   ----
3. Siciliana [arr. Respighi]   Anon. 16th Century
4. La Gueuse   Couperin
5. Tambourin   Rameau

II
THE SHAPE OF MODERN THINGS. . .

1. Minor Seconds and Major Sevenths 2. Unison
3. Syncopation 4. Ostinato [all from "Mikrokosmos"]   Bartók

Intermission

. . . AND NEW SHAPES PROJECTING

Episode 1   Without Music
Episode 2   -------------

III
DANCES

1. C Major   Music Unpublished
2. F minor   ----- -----------
3. D minor   ----- -----------
4. A minor   ----- -----------

Steinway Piano

Second Concert, Thursday, July 25th, at 8:30 P.M. Piano Recital by
Carol Robinson, member of the Faculty. Program includes Brahms
Sonata in F minor, Works by Bach, Mozart, Scarlatti, Ravel, Bartók,
Strawinsky, Satie and De Falla.

Mary Young Theatre   Centerville, Mass.

Example 6, *Chorale Dance for Elizabeth Delza*, mm. 1-18.

At Gurdjieff's Institute at Fontainbleau, Robinson also established a close friendship with a Montenegrin named Olgivanna. After she married Frank Lloyd Wright, Olgivanna initiated Gurdjieff-like music and exercises for the architectural students, still a regular activity at Taliesin. Robinson became a frequent visitor at Taliesin East and later West, participating in the summer chamber music festivals, fostering the cultural life by giving a solo recital every Sunday, and playing as willingly with amateurs (whom Wright called his "farmer-labor ensemble") as with other professional guests (such as harpist Marcel Grandjany).[17] She managed to conform to the stilted "rules" of the Fellowship—only formal address was allowed, even between married couples—and no one was permitted to walk on the Oriental rug except Carol, who had to cross it to reach the piano. She was in residence at Taliesin West when Wright died at the age of 90 ("unexpectedly," says the *Leschetizky Bulletin* in reporting Robinson's presence[18]). She revised her recital plans to play instead a memorial concert of the architect's favorite works (older, largely Romantic, composers, since Wright had declared the moderns fugitives from great music[19]).

Several Christmas carols among Robinson's compositions may have been intended for Taliesin; Mrs. Wright describes how the singing of carols became a favorite tradition.[20] More specifically, Robinson inscribed a setting of *To Spring* (TTBB) "To the Taliesin Singers," its words from Wright's favorite poet William Blake, its musical style in the late Romantic idiom the architect favored (Appendix B, p. 197). From Blake too came the words of her solo song, *The Lamb* (Appendix B, p. 167). Making the piano here a support for the voice, Robinson combined elements of chromaticism and whole-tone construction. Other composers worked a fascination with the unity and contrast of whole-tone and chromatic elements into large canvases in the early twentieth century. Robinson's *The Lamb* affirms how this musical issue engaged the attention of thoughtful musicians continents away from one another in the contemporary world.

In December 1945, Robinson composed a piano work, *Legend*, for the pianist Harriet Todd. Miss Todd's manuscript is penned but preserves Robinson's added pencilled markings—fingerings, pedallings, and directions such as "easy," "rubato," "*Dolce*," and so forth. *Legend* explores the deep registers of the piano with full-spread chords requiring a pianist of secure and certain touch. There is a notable freedom of movement among points of tonal stability. The work begins in A minor; toward its final high point the music moves, through chromatic alterations, into C minor. With the harmonic minor scale the apparent basis, the composer finds her way from this C minor ultimately into C major

(Appendix B, p. 206). There is a confidence and joy about *Legend* that seems to come from Robinson's delight in composing for her friends.

Another solo piano work, *Pastorale*, emphasizes the Aeolian mode in its chordal structure and in its prevailingly white-note melody. In an age of such radical systems as the twelve-tone method, which she herself taught, Robinson's own search for alternative musical sources veered toward the world of modality. Her music suggests that the musical and philosophical world of Gurdjieff where she found spiritual salvation held, in her view, the greatest hope for the contemporary musical world as well.

Besides composing for her friends, Robinson made creating music a vital part of her students' lives. She regularly composed pieces for them to play—duets for joint efforts, inventions for solo work, etudes to develop their technical skills (*Left Hand Study* and etudes for legato double thirds and selected formal designs, for example), and especially, works to enhance their expressive playing. Elizabeth Delza explains that through such compositions Robinson conveyed her own extraordinary ability to "hear" music to her pupils. "I have never," exclaimed Delza in regard to Robinson's teaching-composing, "encountered *any*thing like it." While musicologists will undoubtedly point out that Robinson's music does not "advance" our ideas of composition harmonically or in other measurable dimensions, what cannot be gauged is the way in which, through compositions specifically designed for students' needs, she brought her students to discern differences in the way one hears and plays Bach and Bartók, Chopin and Stravinsky, Beethoven and Ives.

Robinson encouraged her pupils to compose themselves—and when even the youngest showed such inclination, she preserved their melodies in duets or harmonized chorales, recording the student composer and the successful performance of their efforts. And she wrote music for important events in their lives. When her pupil Gloria Caruso married Michael Hunt Murray, Robinson composed a song, *The Daisies*, to a James Stephens poem. The voice is given its usual declamatory care, and the harmonic scheme, founded in E major, is perhaps most distinguished by the "out of key" singing of the poem's lark in F (Appendix B, p. 164).

From prelude to pedagogical exercise, from Fiona Macleod to feminist texts, from Blake to contemporary spiritual thought, Robinson's music conveys more eloquently than any diary engaging ideas in American life. If she did not always translate those ideas into compositons of enduring quality, her very expression of them proves valuable for understanding the twentieth century. As her friend Frank Lloyd Wright once observed: "Work, great or small—as human expression—must be studied in relation to the time in which it insisted upon its virtues and got itself to human view."[21]

One looks in vain for many of these ideas in current music history books, which largely treat other lives, other musics than these. To read published sources and then to discover Robinson's experience is to wonder if there were not two Americas, each with a different history. Put another way, Robinson forces us to acknowledge the fragmentation endemic to twentieth-century life—whether in the realm of art, science, or technology. Ultimately, the most valuable thing about Robinson's music—and her life—may be the wholeness of the view we retrieve through her story—the intimate connections among the men and women responsible for Western civilization's intellectual life, the matters that claimed their attention, and the context in which they created. In the following pages, we shall see, through Robinson's varied activities and her many friendships, some of the ways in which these ideas travelled—across Asia, Europe, and America.

NOTES

1. Robinson lists these teachers in the biographical entries that she supplied for the Dalcroze School of Music *Bulletins* from 1952 through 1957. Her obituary in *The New York Times*, February 28, 1979, mentions study with Nadia Boulanger, but neither her papers nor memories of family and friends confirm this. Perhaps confusion arose because of another avenue of study she pursued at Fontainebleau, explained below.

    Weidig (1867-1931) supplied biographical details for several Chicago programs on which he appeared, one of which remains with Robinson's papers (18 and 19 February 1921, GU MS 300, Box 4, Folder Chicago: Orchestra Hall, pp. 11-15). Florence Ffrench gives additional information in *Music and Musicians in Chicago* (1899; reprint, New York: Da Capo, 1979), pp. 212-213, as does the *Dictionary of American Biography*, Authors edition, 19: 606.

    Carl Milton Beecher (1883-1968) studied at Northwestern University where he eventually taught from 1913 until 1935. A pianist who also studied with Josef Lhevinne in Berlin, Beecher composed chiefly for piano. Ruth Anderson includes him in *Contemporary American Composers, A Biographical Dictionary*, 2d ed. (Boston: G. K. Hall, 1982), p. 36.

2. Clipping in GU MS 300, Box 4, Folder Chicago.

3.   *Fannie Bloomfield Zeisler, An Appreciation* (Chicago: 1927), p. 32. Robinson's *Intermezzi* have not been found.

4.   Promotional pamphlet "Carol Robinson Pianist," 1921, family papers of Phoebe Sells.

5.   De Luxe Reproducing Roll #C7471.

6.   A success in 1918 that Robinson proudly indicated on her title page: "1st prize National contest," she wrote, underlining "national."

7.   Gilman's letter appears in *William Sharp (Fiona Macleod): A Memoir*, compiled by his wife Elizabeth A. Sharp (London: William Heinemann, 1910), pp. 391-392.

8.   Mrs. Sharp quotes a letter, ibid., pp. 389-390, from Edward Mac-Dowell addressed to "Miss Fiona MaCleod" [*sic*] in which the composer asks permission to dedicate a composition to the poet. According to Marjorie Lowens, author of "The New York Years of Edward MacDowell" (Ph.D. diss., University of Michigan, 1971), the intended dedication never materialized, although the composer seems to have had in mind his *Piano Sonata no. 4* (known as the *Keltic*, Op. 59).

9.   Louise Welch, *Orage with Gurdjieff in America* (Boston: Routledge and Kegan Paul, 1982), pp. 60-61.

10.   Lina Mainiero, ed., *American Women Writers. A Critical Reference Guide from Colonial Times to the Present* (New York: Frederick Ungar Publishing Co., 1979), 1: 523-526.

11.   There is an enormous quantity of literature on Gurdjieff, much of which has been compiled by J. Walter Driscoll and The Gurdjieff Foundation of California in *Gurdjieff, An Annotated Bibliography* (New York: Garland Publishing, 1985). A film entitled *Meetings with Remarkable Men*, directed by Peter Brook with music by Laurence Rosenthal (c. 1978), depicts Gurdjieff's early life with arrangements of his music.

12.   Gorham Munson, *The Awakening Twenties* (Baton Rouge: Louisiana State University Press, 1985), p. 257.

13.   So Louise Welch reports in *Orage with Gurdjieff in America*, pp.
      8, 9, 40. Numerous people relate that Gurdjieff had a way "of
      pressing people's buttons to make them confront their weaknes-
      ses." One remembers that when Robinson played her favorite de
      Falla piece, *Ritual Fire Dance*, Gurdjieff dismissed her talent with
      an off-hand remark. Vanity and ambition, Robinson seems to have
      felt, demanded her inner "work."

14.   Welch, *Orage with Gurdjieff in America*, p. 41.

15.   Thomas de Hartmann, *Musique Pour les Mouvements de G.I.
      Gurdjieff* (Paris: Éditions Janus, 1950). A friend of Russian
      painter Wassily Kandinsky, Hartmann (1885-1956) undertook to
      compose the music for that artist's multi-media theater work *Der
      Gelbe Klang*. Hartmann also contributed an article, "Über
      Anarchie in der Musik," to Kandinsky's *Der Blaue Reiter* (1912):
      88-94. Gunther Schuller has reconstructed *Der Gelbe Klang* from
      Hartmann's sketches, and the world première took place in
      February 1982 at the Marymount Manhattan Theatre in con-
      junction with the Guggenheim exhibition "Kandinsky in Munich,
      1896-1914." See *Arnold Schoenberg, Wassily Kandinsky, Letters,
      Pictures and Documents*, ed. Jelena Hahl-Koch; trans. John C.
      Crawford (London: Faber and Faber, 1984), pp. 157-159, 191;
      and *Gunther Schuller. A Bio-Bibliography*, Bio-Bibliographies in
      Music, no. 6 (Westport, Connecticut: Greenwood Press, 1987).

16.   Delza's reputation as an outstanding educator grew over the years,
      and other musicians sought her out. For ten years she taught at
      the Walden School; together with Gorham Munson, for a time
      Lecturer at the New School for Social Research, and Oscar
      Zeigler, she gave programs of music, dance, and poetry; she
      interpreted Couperin and Rameau, Skryabin and Scarlatti. Delza
      often taught movement to singers, including Judith Raskin. More
      on Delza may be found in *Who's Who in America*, 44th ed., s.v.
      "Delza," and Gorham Munson, *The Awakening Twenties*, pp. xiii-
      xiv, et passim. I am deeply grateful for Delza's encouragement
      and assistance during this study; she has graciously shared her
      personal letters from Carol Robinson, their joint recital programs,
      and examples of Robinson's music.

17.   Grandjany (1891-1975) was American, though born in Paris. A
      keyboardist as well as harpist, Grandjany played the organ at the
      Sacré-Coeur Basilica during World War I. In 1938 he began

teaching at the Juilliard School where he remained, a uniquely
effective teacher, until shortly before his death. See Ann Griffiths,
"Grandjany, Marcel (Georges Lucien)," in *The New Grove
Dictionary of Music and Musicians*, 7: 635.

18.   *The News Bulletin of the LAA* 17/31 (1959): 17. Carol Robinson's
      notes in the family's possession list the last full program she
      played for Frank Lloyd Wright on 30 March 1959. She recorded
      that she played Sunday, 12 April in the living room [at Taliesin
      West] at the same time Wright's burial services were taking place
      in the chapel at Taliesin, Wisconsin. Her friendship with both
      Olgivanna and Frank Lloyd Wright is further documented in letters
      (including one, undated, in the family's possession from Mr.
      Wright that urges her to come for a long stay) and numerous
      recollections of friends, some of whom still belong to the Taliesin
      Fellowship.

19.   Olgivanna Lloyd Wright, *Frank Lloyd Wright, His Life, His Work,
      His Words* (New York: Horizon Press, 1966), p. 136.

20.   Ibid.

21.   Frank Lloyd Wright, *An Autobiography* (New York: Horizon
      Press, 1977), p. 293.

Carol Robinson. Photograph by Mortimer Offner, New York.

PART II

CAROL ROBINSON AND HER FRIENDS

Carol Robinson's openness to people and ideas led her to befriend some of the most fascinating figures of the twentieth century. Sharing with Carol their artistic responses to the new age, they drew her in silverpoint, they danced to her music, and they wrote about her. Those involved in music composed for her. Her composition teacher, Adolf Weidig, dedicated a *Canzonetta* to Carol, and Carl Beecher created a *Waltz* that she frequently performed.[1]

If these works confirm the enduring popularity of Romanticism, three manuscripts among her University of Georgia papers connect her personally with the twentieth-century's "most ultra" composers—George Antheil, Bohuslav Martinů, and Charles Ives. Antheil's *Jazz Sonata* bears an inscription to Carol Robinson in the composer's hand; her students recall that she had known and valued him as a friend. Two folios composed by Bohuslav Martinů preserve a keyboard gem generally unknown to the musical world; friends remember that Martinů sent the music to Robinson. And Charles Ives himself authorized her to perform his *Third Sonata for Piano and Violin*, preserved in photostatic copy in MS 300. These compositions, which individually make important chapters in the history of their respective creators, also put us in close touch with issues critical at the time each was played by Carol Robinson.

NOTES

1. The *Waltz* (in B, or B-flat, minor) is known only from mention on Robinson's programs. A version of *Canzonetta*, inscribed "For Carol Robinson," appears in GU MS 300, Box 3, Folder 2, transcribed for two pianos by Orvis Ross. Ross and Mary Ellen Malkasian performed *Canzonetta* 27 February 1966 in a program of music for two pianos at the Rochester Art Center as a tribute to Weidig, also Ross's teacher. The program states that the work was originally published as a piano solo by Summy and allowed to go out of print, but notes that "Mr. Ross rescued it by lovingly arranging it for two pianos." Ross presented it here as one of *Three Pieces*: *Canzonetta-Shanty Song-Kentucky Fiddle Tune*. All are marked "first time."

CHAPTER 4

CAROL ROBINSON, GEORGE ANTHEIL,
AND *THE LITTLE REVIEW* CIRCLE

Robinson's connections to George Antheil (1900-1959) almost certainly began through her circle of Chicago friends led by Margaret Anderson. Margaret, who once named her chief fault the "habit of always living in italics," was remembered by her contemporary Janet Flanner in the following way:

> Her profile was delicious, her hair blond and wavy, her laughter a soprano ripple, her gait undulating beneath her snug *tailleur*. The truth was that within her lay the mixture and mystery of her real consistence, in no way like her exterior. Her visible beauty enveloped a will of tempered steel, specifically at its most resistant when she was involved in argument, which was her favorite form of intellectual exercise...[1]

In Chicago, Margaret had founded *The Little Review*, a little magazine of international importance. It had as its aggressive subtitle "A Magazine of the Arts, Making No Compromise with the Public Taste." In its pages she promoted Carol Robinson as pianist; she printed photographs of Man Ray, whose work Carol later came to own; she published poems of Imagist poet Hilda Doolittle (H.D.), one of which Carol composed into song; and she ran advertisements depicting opera star Mary Garden, with whom Carol once toured. *The Little Review*'s finest hour perhaps came when Margaret and her co-editor Jane Heap were tried for pornography. The charge, brought by the United States Post Office for having published James Joyce's *Ulysses* in installments, resulted in a $100.00 fine and a lot of valuable publicity. (Only Mary Garden expressed disappointment that the pair did not go to jail—the true test, she insisted, of the strength of one's beliefs.)

Margaret and Jane's friendship with Carol Robinson began in *The Little Review* days when they publicized her career through their magazine. Together with full-page illustrated advertisements (such as the one in Program 5 depicting "Carol Robinson Foremost American Pianist" endorsing the Steinert piano) and lavish announcements of her upcoming recitals, *The Little Review* editors brought attention to Carol with provocative reviews. "Her playing at present has the clearness and innocence of a brook," Margaret wrote in 1915, "if she can get something of the sea into her feeling she will be big."[2] That they admired her singleminded purposefulness shows in Margaret's choosing Carol to explain Gurdjieff's "Work." "When I first heard of this concentration on a paramount aim," she wrote in *The Unknowable Gurdjieff*,

> I thought of a pianist friend of mine, Carol Robinson, who spends several weeks a year teaching in one of the large American colleges for girls. The first thing she always says to a new group is, 'You must understand that if any of you were really going to become pianists you wouldn't be here.'[3]

Some friends believe that it was Margaret and Jane who urged Carol to relocate to New York, where they themselves eventually moved *The Little Review*. The friendship abided many years. All journeyed to Fontainebleau to study with Gurdjieff. Later, Robinson inherited the charmingly primitive farmhouse at Brookhaven, Long Island, with no electricity and no running water that Anderson shared with Heap and which she describes in *My Thirty Years' War*.[4] And the three women enjoyed many close mutual friends from Kathryn Hulme and Dorothy Caruso to Georgette Leblanc and Ezra Pound.

In 1919 or 1920,[5] Margaret, together with Chicago pianist Alan Tanner, another of Carol's friends, spent the summer at Bernardsville, New Jersey, where they went "to live exclusively on music" in the household of Georgette Leblanc, the actress, singer, and longtime love of Maurice Maeterlinck. The three became friends with George Antheil, then a promising nineteen-year-old with a baby face, an incredibly percussive piano technique, and a burning ambition to become a composer. As Linda Whitesitt explains in her engaging monograph,[6] Antheil subsequently gained a reputation as the most notorious, and for some, the most promising, American composer of the 1920s. His iconoclastic concerts were often highlighted by such antics as locking the doors of the hall and prominently placing a revolver on the piano lid. He appropriately titled his autobiography *Bad Boy of Music*. After a little over a decade in Europe, during which he also wrote frequently, he attracted the attention of actress Hedy Lamarr. The pair eventually collaborated on a radio-directed torpedo for use in World War II, which they jointly patented in 1941.

Program 5. *The Little Review*'s Advertisement for the Steinert Piano, Spring 1924, featuring Carol Robinson

THE STEINERT
──PIANO──

Well before the torpedo venture, however, George Antheil, like Carol Robinson, had been promoted and published by Anderson in *The Little Review* and personally introduced among her intellectual friends. She and Georgette launched Antheil on his European concert tour with a farewell party at Georgette's Greenwich village apartment.[7] In Paris the following summer, Anderson invited the composer to tea with Erik Satie and Ezra Pound.[8] Pound became a devoted propagandist of Antheil, and his book *Antheil and the Treatise on Harmony* (Chicago: 1927) remains a unique document of a curious liaison.[9] Satie's role in Antheil's music awaits full exploration, but the composer may owe some of his music's "strong satirical and ironic sense"[10] to Satie's example. And the seeming *non sequiturs* of some of his music—*non sequiturs* that often work brilliantly—may have been learned from Satie as well.

In the fall of 1923 Margaret Anderson and Georgette Leblanc arranged for Antheil to play his piano sonatas before all of Paris at the opening of the season's most important ballet. Sure that his music would cause a *scandale*, Leblanc planned in advance to film the audience's reactions for her silent film *L'Inhumaine*.[11] Antheil, happily identifying those in the rioting audience as James Joyce, Picasso, *Les Six*, the Polignacs, the Prince of Monaco, the surrealist group, and Man Ray, concluded that the effect of Margaret and Georgette's "trick" was that "one could not announce a concert of mine between autumn 1924 and autumn 1926 without its being sold out far in advance."[12]

In later years Antheil publicly acknowledged Anderson's role in his life. "I adored Margaret," he wrote,

> and, viewed from 1946, she undoubtedly had a very great influence upon my earliest ambitions, for through her I first became acquainted with the entire contemporary world—sacks of mail came into the house at Bernardsville from all over the world, but particularly from London and Paris, bearing manuscripts, reproductions of new paintings, news of art movements, among these manuscripts of Jean Cocteau and Ezra Pound.[13]

Certainly, Margaret together with Jane Heap had kept the art world's attention on George Antheil. *The Little Review* editors announced his music's first performances and printed his articles; reproduced both his *Airplane Sonata* and his picture as contemporary iconography; publicized his collaboration with Fernand Leger (whose own paintings and ideas about machine aesthetics appeared in *The Little Review*); and even squabbled publicly with the composer.[14] For, despite their evident attempts to promote the young unknown, Antheil at times exhibited that childish and petulant behavior that sustains the image of the "bad boy" who never grew up. His letters in late 1923 and 1924 ill-temperedly refer to Anderson as a *former* friend and angrily denounce *The Little Review*, listing it second among the "things I hate"; meanwhile, he accused Jane of "swiping his ideas" about Stravinsky's *Les Noces*.[15]

His diatribes do not explain this sudden peevishness. Hugh Ford, in his entertaining *Four Lives in Paris*, attributes George's irritation to Georgette Leblanc's performances of his songs which, George charged, capitalized unfairly on the composer's reputation.[16] Perhaps his behavior stemmed from his annoyance with Jane over a freight-load of paintings left to George by a Russian friend.[17] Jane initially agreed to pay the trans-Atlantic freight to enable George to ship them home. When the paintings arrived, however, their cost exceeded almost five times the projected price, and Heap, unable to pay, appealed to George for help. Antheil, destitute as usual, in turn wrote Mrs. Bok and asked her to intervene.

Mrs. Bok herself may have turned George against *The Little Review* circle. His chief source of financial support, Mary Louise Curtis Bok did not at all admire Antheil's friends. In the late 'twenties Antheil assured her he had "left Paris and the friends you speak of, forever" after a letter in which Mrs. Bok had lamented "I don't care for the group you quote, nor their work . . . Pound, Joyce, and so forth."[18] In later correspondence Bok was even more specific.

> I am trying to read 'Ulysses' that you rate so highly [which *The Little Review* had first published in America and on whose chapter "Cyclops" Antheil had once thought of writing an opera], and again see no reason in the line of argument that for strength one must, along with strong, fine things, drag in things that it is bad taste to dwell upon. It is offensive, and one need not be offensive to evidence strength.[19]

Nevertheless, in the closing issue of *The Little Review*, Antheil's point of view (which Margaret once noted "changed on every subject everyday and still remained interesting"[20]) veered toward the grandiloquent: "I send every bit of admiration I have to both of you," he addressed both Jane and Margaret,

> for your great courage in founding and taking so far the greatest and most historical review of our country and hope that you might accept my love and thanks for all you have

both done for me in the most vital period of my life—when I was twenty.[21]

Probably at this very time—when he was twenty—Antheil came to know Carol Robinson, an emphatic friend of Anderson, Heap, Leblanc, and Tanner, and soon a devoted friend of Antheil. The composer must have sent Robinson a copy of the *Jazz Sonata* from Europe, for her manuscript bears the words "To Carol Robinson with greetings from George Antheil, Berlin, 1923" (Example 7a). If Antheil's changeable statements can be believed, he actually composed the *Sonata* in 1920, the time Margaret was "introducing him to the entire contemporary world." He so claims in a letter to Minna Lederman and notes that he "retouched [it] in Berlin in 1923 for a single public performance."[22]

Carol Robinson performed the *Sonata* at the League of Composers' first Lecture-Recital November 16, 1924, just preceding Olin Downes speaking about "The Younger Generation in Music" (Program 6). She gave it at least one other performance. On April 18, 1926, Robinson played the *Jazz Sonata* in Portland, Oregon, under the auspices of E. Robert Schmitz's Pro-Musica.

The League of Composers' printed records grant the 1924 performance the asterisk they give to world premières, but Antheil's letter to Lederman and several other letters imply that he had already performed it—and to European acclaim.[23] American critics, however, were not impressed. "Poor, posturing stuff," huffed Olin Downes in *The New York Times*, although "intelligently and bravely played . . ."[24] Downes appeared so agitated over the concert that he misreported the pianist as Esther Streicher (who appeared elsewhere on the program) instead of Carol Robinson. Other critics frankly expressed disappointment that the *Jazz Sonata* was not as outrageous as they had anticipated. Lawrence Gilman, of the *Herald Tribune*, complained that it was about as "terrifyingly radical as a meeting of the Board of Governors of the Association for Preserving the Grave of Mendelssohn."[25] Even Aaron Copland, who enjoyed a reputation as an ardent supporter of fellow Americans, publicly dismissed the work in *Modern Music* as "simply a poor restatement of the Stravinsky Piano Rag-Music."[26]

Example 7a. George Antheil, *Jazz Sonata*, title page and dedication, courtesy of the Antheil Estate and the Hargrett Library.

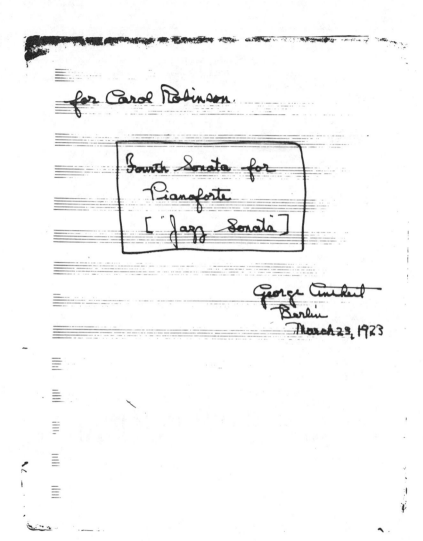

Example 7b. George Antheil, *Jazz Sonata*, mm. 1-12, courtesy of the Antheil Estate and the Hargrett Library.

Program 6. League of Composers First Lecture-Recital

THE LEAGUE OF COMPOSERS, INC.
29 WEST 47th STREET
FIRST LECTURE - RECITAL
SUNDAY, NOVEMBER 16th, 1924
at 3.30 P. M.

N.Y.C.

ANDERSON GALLERIES, Park Avenue and 59th Street

THE PROGRAMME

GEORGES MIGOT—A la memoire de Lili Boulanger (Trio)
MME. ELFRIDA BOOS, JACOB MESTECHKIN
and LEROY SHIELD

CASTELNUOVO-TEDESCO—Nocturne from the suite "Alt Wien"

ERIC FOGG—Two Faery Pieces
        (*a*) Grimm
        (*b*) The Wee Folk's Market
        MME. ESTHER STREICHER

GEORGES ANTHEIL—Jazz Sonata
        MISS CAROL ROBINSON

"The Younger Generation in Music"
MR. OLIN DOWNES

AARON COPLAND—(*a*) Passacaglia
             (*b*) The Cat and the Mouse
        MME. ESTHER STREICHER

BERNARD ROGERS—Two Songs
            (*a*) In the Gold Room
            (*b*) Notturno

RICHARD HAMMOND—Two Songs
              (*a*) Dans les Montagnes
              (*b*) Les trois Princesses
        MME. INEZ BARBOUR
DANIEL LAZARUS—Fantasy

ALOIS HABA—Two Grotesque Pieces

ERNST KRENEK—A Dance Study
LEROY SHIELD

ALEXANDER STEINERT—Three Songs
              (*a*) Lady of the Clouds
              (*b*) Snow of Twilight
              (*c*) Footsteps in the Sand
        MME. INEZ BARBOUR

(Mason and Hamlin Piano)

The November issue of the League of Composers' Review is now available to League
    members, and on sale to the general public.
An international program of contemporary chamber music will be presented at the
    first concert on Sunday night, November 30th at the Klaw Theatre.

OFFICE OF THE LEAGUE OF COMPOSERS
29 West 47th Street.

Stung, Antheil retorted with the letter to *Modern Music*'s editor, Minna Lederman, claiming 1920 as the *Sonata*'s composition date and insisting that the work is "not at all like my present style."[27] Perhaps Copland's own successes coupled with another unfavorable comparison with Stravinsky (Hemingway having noted after hearing Antheil's music that he liked his Stravinsky straight[28]) heaped too much salt into this hyperreactive composer's wounds.

For all his caviling, Antheil's flamboyant and sneering music actually testifies to important artistic issues of the 'twenties. One issue, obviously, was jazz and its perceived importance for enabling a specifically American art music. Antheil's opinions about jazz vacillated as wildly as they did on most other topics. He wrote Mrs. Bok from Berlin that

> American Jazz is the product and FOLKSONG of an enter-prizing [*sic*] and daring blood that has left other lands in the spirit of materialism and dissatisfaction. Jazz is not a craze---------it has existed in America for the last hundred years and continues to exist each year more potently than the last.
>
> As for its artistic significance, the organization of its line, color, & dimension Y....its dynamic & mechanistic significance is that it is one of the greatest artistic land-marks of modern art.[29]

A scant two years later, he exhorted:

> ... the stuff of which music is made is not sound-vibration, but TIME. So it is not a question of new chords one may be inventing, or new musical resources one may be trying to glorify by a more elegant harmony (such as jazz!) but what new projections one is making into musical space...[30]

The very next year he created a *Jazz Symphony*, meanwhile claiming "I hate jazz!"[31]

More convincing than Antheil's kaleidoscopic ruminations is his music. The two known manuscripts of the *Jazz Sonata* bear the dates 1922 and 1923 respectively and disagree chiefly in the greater number of performance details in Robinson's version.[32] In its single movement, the *Sonata* demonstrates how in music, as in life, Antheil readily and una-bashedly changed his mind as freely as he drew breath. Showy glissandos punctuate ragtime rhythms and jazzy seventh chords here; Coney Island

cacophony sounds forth in outrageous dissonances and machine-like os-
tinati there. Like many other Antheil compositions of the 'twenties, and
presumably like Antheil himself, the *Jazz Sonata* has fun by poking fun.

Along with jazz, the *Sonata* attests to Antheil's fascination with
machines and the possibilities they suggested for a more dissonant and
percussive musical language. Antheil instructs the pianist to "play with
even and rapid touch, like a player piano" and writes in a horrifically dissonant language, favoring, for example, left-hand chords in E-flat major
against right-hand harmonies in D major. His dissonances sound the more
jarring as he intersperses them with conventional cadences and Debussy-
like parallelisms and then cynically mocks those "pretties" with discordant
musical jibes, as he does, for instance, at measures 26-36 (Example 8).
In the final pages, Antheil marks a lengthy passage "Brittle and wooden"
before bringing back the main theme in a sonata-like recapitulation. The
final six measures, where "[eighth note]=[quarter] almost," bear three
times the direction *accel!*, with the pianist required to reach for greater
and greater extremes of register as well as speed.

Antheil's own interest in this music of the machine culminated in
the *Ballet mécanique*; after that work he turned to a neoclassicism mo-
delled on that of Stravinsky. Antheil was not alone in his interest in the
aesthetics of the machine: *The Little Review*'s pages reflect similar con-
cerns, and Jane Heap ultimately organized a Machine-Age Exposition,
whose catalogue became *The Little Review*'s 1927 issue.

Example 8. George Antheil, *Jazz Sonata*, mm. 26-36, courtesy of the
Antheil Estate and the Hargrett Library.

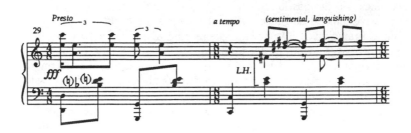

Despite his pronouncement to Minna Lederman that the *Jazz Sonata* was not at all like his present (1925) style, in truth Antheil gave the *Sonata* new life through his *Jazz Symphony*. To understand this connection, some words about the *Jazz Symphony* are in order. A fun-loving and spirited composition, the *Jazz Symphony* exists in several versions, reflecting both the composer's interest in the practicalities of performance and his increasing wariness with the aesthetic of his early works.[33] Apparently the earliest, an orchestral score dated 1925, has in common with the *Jazz Sonata* only its one-movement format, syncopations, and restless allusions to many different twentieth-century sounds. These include a parody of the Soldier's march from *L'Histoire du Soldat*, Ellingtonian muted-trumpet solos (Examples 9 and 10), and, as a surprise ending, a schmaltzy "waltz with Viennese *schwung*, to be played elegantly." Although commissioned by Paul Whiteman, the original *Jazz Symphony* received its first performance by W. C. Handy's Orchestra under Allie Ross.[34] The occasion, New York's Carnegie Hall, April 10, 1927, was to prove a sadly memorable event in George Antheil's life (Program 7). The all-Antheil program, which included the *Jazz Symphony*, the composer's *String Quartet*, and his *Second Sonata for Violin* (with accompaniment of Piano and Drums), culminated with the *Ballet mécanique*. A bawdy backdrop, a mistimed fire siren, and overzealous and poorly directed airplane propellors created havoc.

Example 9, George Antheil, *Jazz Symphony*, rehearsal number 36, courtesy of the Antheil Estate and the Hargrett Library.

Example 10, George Antheil, *Jazz Symphony*, 4 mm. before rehearsal number 53, courtesy of the Antheil Estate and the Hargrett Library.

George Antheil   69

Program 7. George Antheil, Carnegie Hall Concert

CARNEGIE HALL. SUNDAY. APRIL 10. 8:30 P.M.

The Biggest Musical Event of the Year!

GEORGE
ANTHEIL

*Sensational American modernist composer, in his first
American appearance, in a concert of his own works.*

BALLET MECANIQUE
EUGENE GOOSSENS, Conducting

Ten distinguished pianists, George Antheil at the mechanical piano;
eight xylophones, four bass drums; two wind machines, electric
bells, etc., etc.

JAZZ SYMPHONY

W. C. HANDY   GEORGE ANTHEIL
(Originator of the Blues)   at
and his 30-piece orchestra   *the piano*

STRING QUARTET
THE MUSICAL ART QUARTET

SONATA *for Piano,* Violin and Drum
GEORGE ANTHEIL *and* SASCHA JACOBSEN

SCALE OF PRICES			
Tickets now on sale at Carnegie Hall Box Office.	BALCONY $ .75	UPPER TIER BOXES (Seating Eight) $12.00	Baldwin Pianos used throughout the concert.
	DRESS CIRCLE 1.65		Welte-Mignon Piano for mechanical part of
	ORCHESTRA 3.30	LOWER TIER BOXES (Seating Eight) $11.00	Ballet Mecanique.

Personal Management: Donald S. Friede, 61 W. 48th St., New York

Carol Robinson participated in this extraordinary event; of the ten pianos required for the *Ballet mécanique*, she played Piano II. Despite the qualifications and name recognition of the participants, Aaron Copland on Piano I, Colin McPhee and Antheil on other keyboards, Eugene Goossens conducting, Antheil's *Ballet mécanique* set off a rash of ridicule that, two decades later, the composer felt plagued him still. He so confides in his autobiography, and as late as 1949 he bitterly complained to Olin Downes that the latter's "unfair" reviews stemmed from the disastrous performance of the *Ballet mécanique*:

> Underlying your critique [of my Fifth Symphony], mostly, I detect an ancient anger with me concerning the "Ballet Mécanique," my beginnings in Paris (almost thirty years ago!) and a general inability to regard me as I am, not as I was. . . is it not possible that, today, I am merely following out a style and a method of composition which I myself originated—although, of course, I may have been influenced by what has happened since; what composer may not be? I believe that there is a great deal of absolute evidence which, if investigated, would prove that I have at least a fighting and debatable point. In any case, such an investigation would prove that, since 1928 (one year after the Ballet Mecanique concert) I have been following out a line of composition and philosophy from which I have not deflected an inch; and this during a time when most other American composers were following out a highly dissonant and hot-house ivory-tower school of composition and thought (in 1928-35).[35]

Public and critical furor after the Carnegie Hall concert took little notice of other works on the program. The scores show, however, that Antheil eventually took up the *Jazz Symphony* again. The two-piano reduction in the Library of Congress entitled *Jazz Symphony* shows that the composer pared more than 100 measures from the earlier work.[36] More interestingly in this context, he incorporated the *Jazz Sonata's* principal theme. Specifically, the *Sonata's* measures 3-21 now appear as the revised *Jazz Symphony's* second theme (measures 33-45), given over to the orchestra rather than to the piano and recapitulated (as in the *Sonata*) at the close (Example 11).

Example 11, George Antheil, *Jazz Symphony*, revised version, rehearsal
no. 2, courtesy of the Antheil Estate and the Hargrett Library

Linda Whitesitt quotes Virgil Thomson's enthusiasm for this version of the
Jazz Symphony:

> The Jazz Symphony is terrific fun, as always. The tunes,
> in particular are wonderful...Sometime, somewhere I want
> to see it revived, because there is vitality in it.[37]

Thomson's wish came true. In December, 1960, Richard Korn conducted
the *Jazz Symphony*'s revised version at Carnegie Hall. And in a stunning
irony that Antheil would have loved, on July 12, 1989, the original *Jazz
Symphony* was heard again in Carnegie Hall, when Maurice Peress recreated the entire Antheil concert of April 10, 1927.

* * *

Well before Antheil's Carnegie Hall disaster, Carol Robinson had
played the *Jazz Sonata* a second time: in Portland, Oregon, April 18,
1926, under the auspices of the Pro-Musica. Since this program also has
a direct bearing on Bohuslav Martinů's music, it deserves some scrutiny.
The Pro-Musica had been founded by E. Robert Schmitz, a vibrant
pianist born the same year as Carol Robinson, whom *The Little Review*
billed as "the great French conductor and composer." Although originally
calling his organization the Franco-American Musical Society (New York,
1920), Schmitz eventually widened its scope beyond matters French and
American; he wanted "to stimulate and promote a better understanding,
relationship, and co-operation between nations, races, societies and classes
by making available the best of the past, present and future artistic compositions in the field of music and allied arts."[38] Schmitz brought Alfred
Casella and Sergei Prokofiev to tour the United States, sought out Alban
Berg and Egon Wellesz for membership, and succeeded in bringing Maurice Ravel, Ottorino Respighi, Zoltán Kodály and Béla Bartók to America,
a first for each of them. He enlisted prominent persons as directors, including Charles Ives, Mrs. Thomas A. Edison, and Greta Torpadie. To
approve programs, he created an International Advisory Board, whose
members ranged from Bloch and Bridge to Varèse and Weber; to voice
members' interests he initiated a quarterly, the *Pro Musica*, edited by Ely
Jade (actually his wife Germaine).
Portland, Oregon, represents one of more than forty chapters the
energetic Schmitz established across America. Their Second Referendum
Concert—"...exclusively for members. Please present cards at the
door"—took place on Sunday afternoon at a private residence, the home

of Mr. and Mrs. Wells Gilbert (Program 8). The music ranged from piano solos to string quartets, wind ensembles, and combined string and winds. Robinson's first appearance of the afternoon came when she played Stravinsky's four-hand transcription from *Petrouchka* with Ruth Bradley Keiser. Later she performed three keyboard solos: Auric's *Sonatine*, Martinů's *Par T.S.F.*, and Antheil's *Jazz Sonata* which, the program specifies, was "Dedicated to Miss Robinson." That Martinů's autograph also reposes among Robinson's papers brings up the question of how Carol Robinson came to own Bohuslav Martinů's music. It is to this question that we now turn our attention.

Program 8a. Pro-Musica. Second Referendum Concert

PRO-MUSICA, Inc., Portland Chapter
Formerly Franco-American Musical Society, founded 1920.

Second Referendum Concert

At the Residence of
Mr. and Mrs. Wells Gilbert, Riverwood

Sunday Afternoon, April 18, 1926, at Three O'clock.
(*Programs are suggested by International Advisory Board*)

Carol Robinson, Pianist
Ruth Bradley Keiser, Pianist

Mme. Frida Stjerna, Soprano
Margaret Notz, Accompanist

STRING QUARTET

Sylvia Weinstein Margulis, First Violin
Marie Chapman Macdonald, Second Violin

Marion Mustee, Viola
Harold Taylor, 'Cello

WIND ENSEMBLE

B. Diehl, First Clarinet
J. Thomson, Second Clarinet

W. Couling, Oboe
B. L. Brown, Bassoon

Margaret Laughton, Flute

Program 8b. Pro-Musica. Second Referendum Concert

PROGRAM

I.

Set of Tunes and Dances....................................Purcell, arr. by Bliss

1. Overture (The Gordian Knot)   3. Saraband (Amphitryon)
2. Air (Distressed Innocence)   4. Minuet (Distressed Innocence)
                    5. Hornpipe (The Married Beau)
                    STRING QUARTET

II.

Petrouchka (transcribed by the composer for piano, 4 hands).............Stravinsky
                    Carol Robinson and Ruth Bradley Keiser

III.

La Boule de Neige...Louis Durey
The Ragwort .... Arthur Bliss
Chanson .... A. Honegger
Cycle Alphabet (three numbers).................................. Georges Auric
                1. Hirondelle   2. Escarpin   3. Filet a' Papillons
                    Mme. Frida Stjerna

IV.

Sonatine .... Auric
                    Allegro — Andante — Presto
"Par T. S. F."...Martinu
Jazz Sonate (Dedicated to Miss Robinson) ....George Antheil
                    Carol Robinson

V.

Impressions of a Department Store (Manuscript) (First Performance)..David Tamkin
                    Dedicated to Mr. Julius L. Meier
                    STRING AND WIND ENSEMBLE
Prelude, 9:15 in the Morning

                    STRING QUARTET
Romance of a Shop Girl

                    WIND QUARTET
Tarantelle, Saturday Afternoon
                    STRING AND WIND ENSEMBLE

This concert is exclusively for members. Please present cards at the door.

NOTES

1. Janet Flanner, "Profile, A Life on a Cloud," *The New Yorker*, 3 June 1974, p. 44.

2. *The Little Review* (May 1915): 50.

3. Margaret Anderson, *The Unknowable Gurdjieff* (New York: Samuel Weiser, [1962]), p. 17.

4. Anderson, *My Thirty Years' War, An Autobiography* (New York: Covici, Friede Publishers, 1930), pp. 184-186.   Robinson's nephew vividly described Carol's summers at the Brookhaven Cottage (LS 23 January 1989): "Each spring she would store both of her pianos with Steinway," he wrote, "sub-let her apartment in NYC, and live the country life.   Many old friends visited her during these summers.   I spent many pleasant times there as a young boy.   Climbing the large elm shown in one of the pictures, roving around the open fields, exploring the tidal water inlet from the Great South Bay.   The inlet came to the very edge of her yard. There was always a leaky row boat in the rushes that I could use. Carol would sometimes get a ride to Bell Port (1-2 miles) for supplies, but most of the time she would walk.   There were no facilities in the cottage.   She cooked on a Kerosene stove, heated with an old Franklin stove she bought for $5.00 at a junk yard, and pumped water from a well at the back of the house.   Perishables such as milk and butter were stored in a root cellar under the house . . . The "OUT HOUSE" was next to some lovely Lilac Bushes.   It was also home for many wasps.   It did not pay to dally."

5. Anderson, who describes meeting Antheil in *My Thirty Years' War*, pp. 235-238, in unforgettable prose, is vague about the year. She remembers that he was 19; he remembers that he was 20. Since George turned 20 on July 8, 1920, perhaps 1920 is the year. Anderson also mentions the composer hard at work setting poems of Adelaide Crapsey.   The published *Adelaide Crapsey Songs* bear the dates 1919-1920.

6. *The Life and Music of George Antheil 1900-1959* (Ann Arbor, Michigan: UMI Research Press, 1983).   I should like to thank Dr. Whitesitt for the valuable additional help she has provided in many telephone conversations.

7.   LC, Antheil-Bok Correspondence, LS George Antheil, 9 November 1922. See also Wayne D. Shirley, "Another American in Paris: George Antheil's Correspondence with Mary Curtis Bok," *The Quarterly Journal of the Library of Congress* 34 (1977): 2-22.

8.   George Antheil, *Bad Boy of Music* (New York: Doubleday, 1945), p. 117.

9.   Bravig Imbs, in his *Confessions of Another Young Man* (New York: Henkle-Yewdale House, 1936), p. 21, observed "He [Antheil] always felt grateful to Pound for the latter's opus, but I thought the gratitude should be the other way around."

10.   George Antheil, Preface to *Sonata No. 4* (New York: Weintraub Music Company, 1951).

11.   Adrienne Monnier gives a first-hand account in *The Very Rich Hours of Adrienne Monnier*, trans. with an introduction and commentaries by Richard McDougall (New York: Charles Scribner's Sons, 1976), pp. 247-249.

12.   *Bad Boy*, p. 137.

13.   Ibid., pp. 116-117.

14.   George Antheil figures in the following *The Little Review* issues: (Autumn-Winter 1923-24): 39; (Spring 1924): 64; (Autumn-Winter 1924-25): 13-15, 42-44; (Spring 1925): 33; (Spring 1929): 14-15.

15.   LC, Antheil-Bok Correspondence, LS George Antheil, ? March 1924, and *The Little Review* (Spring 1924): 64.

16.   Hugh Ford, *Four Lives in Paris*, with a Foreword by Glenway Wescott (San Francisco: North Point Press, 1987), p. 28. Ford devotes an entire chapter to George Antheil.

17.   LC, Antheil-Bok Correspondence, LS George Antheil, ? January 1924. Antheil describes the episode at some length.

18.   Ibid., LS George Antheil, 1 August 1929.

19.   Ibid., CC Mary Curtis Bok, 16 September 1930.

20.   Anderson, *My Thirty Years' War*, p. 238.

21.   *The Little Review* (Spring 1929): 14.

22.   LC, Modern Music Archives, LS George Antheil to Minna Leder-
      man, ? February 1925. Whitesitt, however, notes that the *Jazz
      Sonata* is stylistically consistent with other works of 1923 and in
      keeping with the dates on the known manuscript copies; telephone
      conversation, 23 July 1989.

23.   "The League of Composers. A Record of Performances and a
      Survey of General Activities from 1923 to 1935" (New York: The
      League of Composers, [n.d.]), p. 5; the letter references to the
      Jazz Sonata include that in note 22 above and LC, Antheil-Bok
      Correspondence, LS (February or March, 1923), Berlin: "The last
      few months has seen the completion of three new piano sonatas...
      'Sonata sauvage' in three movements, 'The Death of Machinery'
      in four movements, and 'Jazz Sonata'... a new synthetic jazz
      which has made a tremendous hit here."

24.   *The New York Times*, 17 November 1924, p. 17. Downes's
      lecture does not appear among those of his papers that have been
      classified in GU MS 688.

25.   *New York Herald Tribune*, 17 November 1924, p. 12.

26.   "George Antheil," *Modern Music* 2 (1925): 27.

27.   LC, Modern Music Archives, letter to the editor enclosed in LS
      George Antheil to Minna Lederman, February 1925.

28.   *The Transatlantic Review* 2 (1924): 341.

29.   LC, Antheil-Bok Correspondence, LS Fall 1922 [?]. I have omit-
      ted Antheil's comma between "dimension, Y."

30.   "Abstraction and Time in Music," *The Little Review* (Autumn-
      Winter 1924-25): 15.

31.   Quoted in Whitesitt, *George Antheil*, p. 112.

32.   The 1922 manuscript is part of the Antheil Estate. The Hargrett
      Library manuscript (GU MS 300, the Carol Robinson Collection,
      Music Folder) has a separate title page. At its top appears "for
      Carol Robinson" followed by the title: Fourth Sonata for/Piano-
      forte/["Jazz Sonata"]. Below this the composer wrote "George

Antheil/Berlin/March 23, 1923." The indication "Fourth Sonata" may cause confusion, since in 1948 Antheil composed a different Fourth Piano Sonata for Frederick Marvin and dedicated it to Virgil Thomson (published by Weintraub, 1951). On the GU MS 300 *Jazz Sonata*, at the first page of music, the composer has reiterated the title-page information: in the right-hand corner appear the words "for Carol Robinson/(with greetings from/George Antheil/1923, Berlin)." He wrote the title here as "IV Sonata for Piano/'Jazz Sonata,'" the title that also heads the manuscript in the hands of the Antheil Estate's executor. On that copy, however, someone has scribbled through the Roman numeral and the word "Jazz," while a different hand, identified by Whitesitt, *George Antheil*, p. 201, as that of the composer's wife, has scrawled across the top "Jazz Sonata 1922."

33. Whitesitt, *George Antheil*, pp. 228-229, lists the various *Jazz Symphonies*, including the first version dedicated to Evelyn Friede (1925; Evelyn was the wife of Donald Friede, the producer of Antheil's concert); a revision dated November 7, 1955; incomplete manuscript parts labelled "Concertino in three parts with solo piano"; and a two-piano reduction, a copy of the last located in the Library of Congress. I should like to thank here Maurice Peress who provided a valuable taped performance of the 1925 *Jazz Symphony*.

34. Whitesitt, *George Antheil*, p. 229. Whitesitt also gives a vivid and detailed account of the Carnegie Hall fiasco, pp. 31-41. One of the problems of Antheil's Carnegie Hall concert was that Friede, its producer, was simultaneously being tried in Boston for selling a copy of Dreiser's *An American Tragedy*. Unlike Anderson and Heap, Friede did go to jail. (Friede, incidentally, is also the Friede of Covici, Friede, publishers of Margaret Anderson's first book, *My Thirty Years' War*.)

35. GU MS 688 Correspondence File, LS George Antheil, 11 January 1949.

36. George Antheil, *Jazz Symphony*, [for two pianos], LC photocopy of Holograph Music Manuscripts, Music 3149, item #13.

37. Whitesitt, p. 113.

38.   Vivian Perlis, "Pro-musica," *The New Grove Dictionary of Music and Musicians*, 15: 303-304. Perlis describes Schmitz's organization in greater detail in *Two Men for Modern Music. E. Robert Schmitz and Herman Langinger*, I.S.A.M. monographs, no. 9 (Brooklyn, N.Y.: Institute for Studies of American Music, 1978), p. 12ff.

CHAPTER 5

CAROL ROBINSON AND BOHUSLAV MARTINŮ

Carol Robinson acquired new music because she deliberately sought it out and because she made many friends in the intellectual world. Letters, news clippings, and recital programs confirm that she made six or seven trips to Paris, performing, looking for compositions, and circulating among the intelligentsia. Indicative of the company she kept is a story related by one of her students. Hearing a knock at the door of her Paris apartment one night and a plaintive voice, "Carol, it's Ernest, won't you give me something to eat?", she opened the door to find a half-starved Hemingway. Only one of Carol's literary friends, Hemingway joined Gertrude Stein and Ezra Pound as those she described to friends and students in later years. Among artists she befriended Man Ray, whose *Gardenia* she owned, and Jean Cocteau, of whose works she cherished *Maison de santé, Palm print,* and *Goya.* Lett Haines' *The Railroad Train* and Juan Puni's *Still Life* and his *Street Scene* figured among her belongings. She became a devoted companion to Pavel Tchelichev, who roomed with her Chicago friend, pianist Alan Tanner; Tchelichev gave her *Savonarola, Landscape with House,* and *The Opera.*[1]

Robinson also befriended many composers and musicians. She made trips to Wanda Landowska's villa to participate in her master classes; and she never forgot the memorable evening when she witnessed Emil Sauer ("a great favorite of my teacher") honored at the Sorbonne.[2]

Just as Robinson gravitated to the intellectual center that was Paris, so Bohuslav Martinů (1890-1959) left his Czech homeland in the fall of 1923, bringing his memories of childhood at the top of a Polička belltower and his experiences at the Prague Conservatory to the French capital. He intended to study composition with Albert Roussel in Paris, wanting his

> advice, clarity, moderation, taste, and clear, precise, emotional expression, the characteristics of French art which I had always admired and which I wanted to understand as intimately as possible.[3]

Doubtless, he did not anticipate a rich interaction with Americans nor the necessity of relocating to America in the ultimate chaos of another great war. Born in 1890, Martinů's similarity in age as well as a love of music

must have provided the basis for the friendship that began before 1926 and
that Miss Robinson spoke of still, and with warmth, more than twenty-five
years later.

No one remembers just when or how Martinů and Robinson met,
but the Portland performance of *Par T.S.F.* puts both the date of their
acquaintance and the composition of Martinů's piece before April 18,
1926. Since the printed program specifies "First Performance" only for
David Tamkin's *Impressions of a Department Store, Par T.S.F.* must have
been performed earlier. Certainly, its French title and the paper, with its
blind stamp "E. Ploix, 8 rue Ste. Placide, Paris," suggest the work's
origins in Paris.[4]

Martinů lovers may be amazed to learn that Robinson next played
Par T.S.F. at Woodstock, New York—a place whose very name evokes
images of slightly stoned, often nude, and hairy thousands. Spirited
interaction and experimentation with the "new in arts and letters,"
however, had made Woodstock a landmark well before the August 1969
event that featured Jimi Hendrix. Carol's friend, Gorham Munson,
entitled his Epilogue to *The Awakening Twenties* "Woodstock, 1924." He
recalled "The air [as] fresh and heady with the spirit of poetic adventure,
with the daring of aesthetic experiment."[5] At Woodstock in 1931 George
Antheil would compose his *Six Little Pieces for String Quartet* and Henry
Cowell would derive inspiration from nearby singing school masters.

There, in a rustic concert hall on a wooded tract called the
Maverick, Robinson could expect a fair hearing for the ultramoderns in
an environment that drew artists, writers, actors, and musicians. On
September 19, 1926, in the Sunday Concert series that continues to this
day, Robinson followed Beethoven's *C Major String Trio* with eleven
piano solos in which Brahms, Scarlatti, and Bach-Bauer gave way to
Debussy, Hanson and Stravinsky. As her last four numbers, she played
Satie's *Third Gymnopédie*, Martinů's *Par T.S.F.*, and de Falla's *Andaluza*
and *Ritual Fire Dance* (Program 9). Well before the Boston Symphony
performed *La Bagarre* November 17, 1927, and before Elizabeth Sprague
Coolidge received the *String Quartet* for her Festival at Pittsfield,
Massachusetts, audiences on America's east and west coasts had already
heard the name and music of Bohuslav Martinů. For all its tiny size, *Par
T.S.F.* extends Martinů's contact with Americans and they with him by a
least a year and a half. It also gives to Carol Robinson, rather than to
Serge Koussevitzky and the Boston Symphony Orchestra, the honor of
introducing Martinů to the American musical public.

Program 9. The Maverick Sunday Concerts

THE MAVERICK SUNDAY CONCÊRTS
(Every Sunday at 4 o'clock, d. s. time)

Program for September 19, 1926

CAROL ROBINSON	piano
PIERRE HENROTTE	violin
GAETANE BRITT	violin
HENRY MICHAUX	viola

Trio C maj. op. 87 B   **Beethoven**
  for two violins and viola
  Allegro
  Adagio cantabile
  Menuetto - allegro molto scherzo
  Finale - presto

Piano Solos
  Rapsody Op. 119 No. 4   **Brahms**
  Sonate C minor   **Scarlatti**
  Sonate A major   **Scarlatti**
  Toccata   **Bach - Bauer**

  Delphic Dancers   **Debussy**
  Clog Dance   **Hanson**
  Chez Petrouchko   **Stravinsky**
  Third Gymnopedie   **Satie**
  Par T. S. F.   **Martinu**
  Andaluza   **De Falla**
  Ritual of Fire   **De Falla**

The Maverick uses a Steinway Piano.

Robinson's programs show two additional performances of *Par T.S.F.* before the end of the decade. One took place in New York in May 1929 on the series called "Afternoon musicales with the Bechstein." The other suggests some clues to the life she must have led in Paris. There, on December 29, 1928, Robinson played Martinů's music at the U. S. Students and Artists' Club. Connected with St. Luke's Chapel of the American Church of the Holy Trinity, the Club offered a library, radio and piano, billiard rooms, hot and cold showers, and current newspapers, chiefly to English-speaking men. On certain days, however, women were permitted to join in, and on Sundays at 8:45 the American Women's University Club provided a "Musical Evening." "Community singing and a social hour will conclude the program," promised the *New York Herald Tribune*'s Paris edition in announcing Carol Robinson's upcoming performance.[6]

If *Par T.S.F.* suggests that Robinson found the club network as useful in Paris as it had proved in America, it also shows the fruitful results of interaction between Carol and her artistic friends. When Robinson introduced Elizabeth Delza to Martinů's miniature, the dancer was so delighted with the Czech's invention that she proceeded to choreograph *Par T.S.F.* for her New York debut, which took place at the Guild Theatre on March 12, 1933[7] (see Program 10).

Martinů titled his piece after an important issue of the 'twenties. *Par T.S.F.* or *Par télégraphie sans fils* means "across the wireless" or "on the radio." Just at the time Martinů arrived in France, Parisian periodicals reverberated with excitement over radio's musical possibilities. In 1924, Étienne Royer, writing on "La Musique et la T.S.F." in *La Revue Musicale*, addressed some of the reservations musicians expressed about the radio:

> Parmi les musiciens, un assez grand nombre commencèrent
> à considerer la radiophonie avec un sentiment d'hostilité
> [among musicians, a rather large number began to view
> wireless telephony with a feeling of hostility].[8]

He reassured readers who feared that radio might diminish concert attendance or even replace live performances altogether, pointing out that radio's annoying interruptions, unwanted frequencies, and lack of clarity had so far kept such a thing from happening. By July 1930, Henri Prunières and André Coeuroy devoted one entire issue to *La musique mécanique*, its lead article entitled "La Musique et la T.S.F."[9] R. Raven-Hart began this discussion by considering music and *la T.S.F.* from two points of view: radio broadcasts of existing works and music written specifically for radio.

Program 10a. Elizabeth Delza with Dance Group

ELIZABETH

DELZA
with
dance group

MME. ANNA MEITCHIK
CONTRALTO

CHARLES POSNAK
AT THE PIANO

GUILD THEATRE
52ND ST. WEST OF BROADWAY
● SUNDAY
Mar. 12, 1933
● 8:30 P. M.

Photograph by Leo T. Hurwitz

Program 10b. Elizabeth Delza with Dance Group

I.

1. Bach .... Sinfonia (Partita II)
   ELIZABETH DELZA with Katherine Cane, Mary Cane, Ruth Kramberg, Etille Sorella
2. Lully .... Air Tendre
   ELIZABETH DELZA
3. Unknown (16th Century) .... Siciliana
   ELIZABETH DELZA with Katherine Cane and Mary Cane
4. Pachelbel _____ Eughetta (in Three Voices)
   ELIZABETH DELZA
5. Handel .... Passacaglia (Suite VII)
   ELIZABETH DELZA and Group
6. Couperin .... La Geuse
   ELIZABETH DELZA
7. Rameau .... Tambourin
   ELIZABETH DELZA and Group

II.

C. Hubert Parry.......................... Cycle of Seven Episodes from the Book of Job
   ELIZABETH DELZA and Group

III.

1. Brahms .... Intermezzo, Op. 117, No. 1
   ELIZABETH DELZA and Mary Cane
2. Moussorgsky .... Le Chef d'Armèe (from Songs and Dances of Death)
   ELIZABETH DELZA and Group
   MME. MEITCHIK, contralto
3. Scriabin .... a. Etude   b. Prélude   c. Flammes Sombres
   ELIZABETH DELZA
4. Toch .... Andante
   ELIZABETH DELZA with Katherine Cane and Mary Cane
5. Bartok .... Dirge
   ELIZABETH DELZA
6. Honegger .... Pièce Brève
   ELIZABETH DELZA
7. Martinu .... Allegretto
   ELIZABETH DELZA with Katherine Cane, Mary Cane, Ruth Kramberg
8. Poulenc .... Mouvements Perpétuels
   Group
9. Poulenc .... Valse
   ELIZABETH DELZA

(Steinway Piano)

CONCERT MANAGEMENT: NBC ARTISTS SERVICE, 711 FIFTH AVE., N. Y. GEORGE ENGLES, MANAGING DIRECTOR

NBC ARTISTS SERVICE 711 Fifth Ave., New York City Tel. Plaza 3-1900, Ext. 339	Orchestra—AA through J.................$2.75 Orchestra—Balance ....2.20 Mezzanine—Entire ....2.20 Balcony—E through H.....................1.65 Balcony—Balance 1.10

Enclosed please find check of $ .... for .... tickets at .... each,
for dance recital of ELIZABETH DELZA at Guild Theatre, on Sunday evening, March 12, 1933.
Name .... Address............................

TICKETS NOW ON SALE AT BOX OFFICE

Martinů's piece may not exactly fall into either category, since it appears to evoke programmatically radio's beginnings. A persistent and dry ostinato suggests Morse code, the signal which both telegraphy and early radio transmitted. For sixty seconds the music crackles with staccato and surges and dies with dynamic swells, evoking the erratic splutter of the early wireless. Tone clusters vividly suggest multiple, unwanted frequencies, erupting occasionally into pure, accented octaves. The near-perpetual whole-step motive, ingeniously syncopated in its placement on the sixteenth-note off-beat, unifies measures that succeed each other in almost constantly changing meters (Example 12). Martinů has channeled his familiar ostinatos and homophonies into a toccata to telegraphy. Among the composer's keyboard compositions of the 'twenties, many have the stylistic features of homophony, tone clusters, and toccata-like rhythms, but few sparkle as does this piece.[10]

Scholars usually date Martinů's interest in radio from 1935, when the Czech composed two operas for radio broadcast, *The Voice in the Forest* and *Comedy on the Bridge*. In a few swift measures, *Par T.S.F.* shows Martinů's alertness to the new technology as much as a decade before these operas. It bears eloquent musical testimony to the observation of the composer's friend, Pierre Octave Ferroud, who wrote in 1937:

> This musician who, at first sight, appears to despise space and time is, nevertheless, one of the first to understand the importance of broadcasting and the value of the resources, hitherto unknown, which it puts within the reach of all.[11]

That the composer should make a gift to a pianist friend of a work called "Across the Wireless" brings up the question of Robinson's role in turning her new friend's attention to technology. Although written records have proved elusive,[12] friends and family remember that Robinson served as a telecommunications person in World War I. "That," she emphatically observed to one, "had something to do with music, so I volunteered to do Morse code." Martinů, whose prolifically produced works include those with friends' specific talents in mind, such as the charming *Avec un doigt [A trois mains]* (with one finger [for three hands]), dedicated to "Monsieur and Madame Michel Dillard and to little Jean-Pierre," perhaps intended *Par T.S.F.* as a kind of homage to a woman who communicated as eloquently through her piano keys as through her telegraph key. If the composition itself seems minuscule, just thirty-eight measures, its history and musical personality nonetheless reveal fascinating and unsuspected dimensions of both composer and pianist and puts each at the forefront of musical thinking in their time.

Example 12, Bohuslav Martinů, *Par T.S.F.*, mm. 1-18, courtesy of the Hargrett Library.

NOTES

1. Robinson's nephew David kindly provided the list of paintings, prints, and drawings that were given Carol by the artists or their friends; (those who knew her often remarked that, while the pianist seldom purchased things for herself, her friends gave her many beautiful gifts). Other works in David Robinson's list include David Sterenberg, *Still Life*; George Grosz, *Battleship* and *City View*; Constantin Terechkovitch, *Still Life*; and Jerome Blum, *China 1917*.

2. LS Carol Robinson, writing to Elizabeth Delza, 21 July [1969] remembered: "When the Germans occupied Paris she [Landowska] escaped to this country with only a handbag...Her library and her museum collection of instruments were rescued from the German salt mines by our GIs at end of war." The reference to Sauer appears in her letter to Jean Réti-Forbes, 21 September [no year], GU MS 912, correspondence "Rho-She."

3. B[ohuslav] Martinů, "Témoignage tchécoslovaque," *La Revue musicale* 18 (Numéro special . . . à la mémoire d'Albert Roussel) (1937): 366.

4. Introductory remarks to the Panton edition of *Par T.S.F.* address the manuscript's orthographic details; the edition also includes a facsimile of Robinson's manuscript. See Bohuslav Martinů, *Par T.S.F.*, ed. Glenda Dawn Goss (Prague: Panton Press, 1990).

5. Gorham Munson, *The Awakening Twenties* (Baton Rouge: Louisiana State University Press, 1985), p. 299. Alf Evers, a Catskill neighbor of Henry and Sidney Cowell, traces the artistic fortunes of Woodstock in *The Catskills. From Wilderness to Woodstock* (Woodstock, N.Y.: The Overlook Press, 1982). The famous Woodstock Festival of 1969, which actually took place in Bethel, New York, some fifty miles from the art colony, traded on the latter's already established fortunes by using the Woodstock name.

6. *New York Herald Tribune*, Paris Edition, 29 December 1928, p. 5; clipping in GU MS 300, Box 1, Folder 10.

7.   The Guild Theatre program, "Elizabeth Delza with Dance Group,"
        lists Martinů's work by its tempo *Allegretto*, but the copy in the
        dance company's repertory, probably made by Delza herself from
        Robinson's original, shows that the music was indeed *Par T.S.F.*
        With Charles Posnak at the piano, Delza interpreted the music
        with three other dancers. At least twice during the 1950s, May 6,
        1957 in New York City, and April 22, 1959 at Fairleigh Dickinson
        University, four of her pupils again danced the *Allegretto* as an
        ensemble, first with Raymond Lewenthal, later with John M.
        Schlenck at the piano.

8.   Étienne Royer, "La Musique et la T.S.F.," *La Revue musicale* 5
        (1924): 157-158.

9.   Ibid., 11 (1930).

10.   Theo Hirsbrunner surveys the early keyboard works (minus *Par
        T.S.F.*) in "Bohuslav Martinu: Die Soloklavierwerke der Dreis-
        siger Jahre," *Archiv für Musikwissenschaft* 39 (1982): 64-77.

11.   Pierre Octave Ferroud, "A Great Musician of Today, Bohuslav
        Martinů," *The Chesterian* 18 (1937): 92.

12.   According to John Gerfen, Chief of Records Reconstruction
        Branch, only women who were army nurses were enlisted in
        military service in World War I; other personnel served in a
        civilian capacity. The military's Civilian Personnel Records in St.
        Louis, Missouri, have no record of Carol Robinson, but not all
        documents from World War I have survived. David Robinson
        recalls that his aunt belonged to the Signal Corps and trained in
        New Jersey, where she learned to teach Morse code.

CHAPTER 6

CAROL ROBINSON AND AN AMERICAN MUSICAL IDENTITY

In 1908 a little-known Connecticut Yankee fashioned a work for piano and violin from some organ preludes and a ragtime piece. Having previously encountered opposition from performers, the composer decided to have a "great" musician read through his earlier works for violin before finishing. The "great" turned out to be "a typical hard-boiled, narrow-minded, conceited prima donna solo violinist" whose distress with the horrible sounds led the composer in despair to exclaim "Are my ears on wrong?" and to make alterations in the new sonata in an "attempt to please the soft-ears and be good."[1]

Somewhat later a musician made of tougher mettle and one of the few the composer considered a friend, violinist David Talmadge, played all the composer's works for piano and violin with their composer at the piano. Although he teased about "those funny sounds . . . he gave them serious, hard, and intelligent study, and played them well and in a kind of big way."[2] In 1917 Talmadge and another daredevil, pianist Stuart Ross, tackled the soft-eared piece, now called *Third Sonata for Piano and Violin*. Although the pianist grumbled that it was the "hardest music he had ever played," the pair performed for a small, invited audience at prestigious Carnegie Chamber Music Hall.[3] Thereafter, the *Sonata* disappeared from the performance repertory. The composer himself derogated the sonata "in a slump back" in typically feminine terms as "a weak sister."[4]

Almost three decades later, Carol Robinson discovered the composer, Charles Ives (1874-1954). In 1946, Robinson, with violinist Madeleine Carabo-Cone, initiated a concert series of American chamber music (Program 11). The pair gave four performances of the *Third Sonata for Piano and Violin*, including the "first New York performance" at Town Hall (the two were evidently unaware of the Carnegie Chamber Music occasion in 1917). In 1947 Robinson and Cone performed the work again in the Brooklyn Museum Concert series and in 1948 in Times Hall. Robinson was not the first to resurrect the *Third Sonata*—Sol Babitz and Ingolf Dahl had performed it on the west coast earlier in 1946—but her repeated performances, her personal enthusiasm for Ives, and her articulate explanations of the music contributed to the public's growing awareness of the composer.

Program 11. Contemporary American Program

MADELEINE **CARABO**
VIOLINIST

assisted by

CAROL **ROBINSON**
PIANIST

TOWN HALL

Nov. 11th, Monday Afternoon, 5:30 P.M.

Contemporary American Program

Three First New York Performances

Third Violin Sonata by CHARLES E. IVES

Sonata by HAROLD S. CONE

Sonata by ROY HARRIS

RECENT PRESS COMMENTS

"Miss Carabo played with technical skill and a good quality of tone, as well as **INTERPRETIVE INSIGHT."**
                                    —New York Herald-Tribune, June 2, 1946

" . . . Miss Carabo's playing boasted inner warmth and coloring — in readings spirited, clean-cut and rhythmically secure — provided the chance for an evocation of communicative and contrasting moods that were well defined in able interpretations."
                                    —New York Times, June 2, 1946

Robinson's chamber music series illustrates a tendency so widespread throughout America that in retrospect historians speak of "an American wave" in music from 1930 until the mid-1940s. Wiley Hitchcock identifies the themes of these years as "a conservative trend, a historical or regional Americanism and a search to reach a broader public."[5] Along with the rediscovery of Charles Ives as an American original, Wiley cites the manifestations of these trends as the "finds" of "earlier American music, especially the eighteenth-century New England singing-school music and American folk music in general."[6] Robinson's chamber music programs of the 'forties might have served Hitchcock as a model for these abstractions, for along with resurrecting Ives, she and Carabo-Cone gave New Yorkers the premières of two other American sonatas: Henry Cowell's, inspired by the eighteenth-century singing school tradition and Roy Harris's, which incorporates an American folk tune. They also performed Ulysses Kay's *Sonatina for Violin and Piano* (composed 1942), and Carabo-Cone with her husband Harold Cone premiered the latter's *Violin Sonata*.

That nearing sixty Carol Robinson still dauntlessly tackled music that deterred most performers testifies to her still youthful, pioneering spirit. The rewards were few; the principal critics, Virgil Thomson at the *Herald Tribune* and Olin Downes at *The New York Times*, did not cover her programs; although *Herald Tribune* critic Arthur Berger gave both musicians credit for "selflessly devoting themselves to three premiers,"[7] he objected to their choices of music. Often the reviewers did not mention the pianist at all, directing their compliments and their criticisms to the violinist alone. Given the prominent role of the piano, especially in Ives's *Sonata* (perhaps the reason he called it *Sonata for Piano and Violin*, not the more usual "Violin Sonata"), such oversight reveals a deplorable lack of sensitivity and musical understanding. In later years Carol herself expressed her vexation; in a letter to Jean Réti-Forbes, she confided that Carabo-Cone had received top billing in their chamber series: "I was always in smaller type" [literally, "tape"] and though she was a "very brilliant delightful friend, not a very good violinist because she does not practice!"[8] This explanation perhaps accounts for the less than enthusiastic reception the sonatas received from the critics.

* * *

Despite her capacity for friendship, Robinson probably never met Charles Ives. Partly out of concern for his health, partly from the composer's idiosyncratic views of musicians, Ives and his wife Harmony

isolated themselves from outsiders.[9] Nevertheless, some written com-
munications flowed between Carabo-Cone and Robinson and the composer
and his wife. The musicians received a copy of the music; no great favor,
some would aver, for the very appearance of those photostats, Frank
Rossiter observes, "was enough to frighten away all but the dedicated."[10]
Despite his earlier grousing about the "weak sister," Ives expressed
pleasure in the *Sonata*'s performance by "those who, like you, feel and
understand what is behind it all."[11] He communicated through Harmony
("As you know I write for Mr. Ives who is not well and it is difficult for
him to do so"[12]). Mrs. Ives continued "their" letter with remarks about
the music. Carol, who made the program notes for the concerts, as the
drafts in her hand rest with her other notes, supplemented the information
supplied by the Iveses with her own insights.

Mrs. Ives explained that the first movement "was partly from some
of Mr. Ives' earlier music, a piece for organ and voice which was played
in an organ recital at the Central Presbyterian Church, New York, in
1902."[13] Carol repeated this information almost verbatim in her program
notes; ever the teacher, she added an explanation of the first movement's
form: "composed of four sections, each labeled 'stanza' and culminating
in a refrain. Each section," she wrote, "treats of the same hymn material
[identified in her score as 'Beulah Land'] in a different way, and each
seems to reveal the tune more transparently." Her notes continue:

> Similarly, in the final movement "I Need Thee Every
> Hour" sounds forth at the end in much of its original form
> and the middle movement furnishes an appropriate contrast
> in which elements of ragtime and other lively rhythms
> make for an indigenous type of scherzo. A pencilled
> footnote to the piano score of this Allegro reads "This
> would be easier for four hands."

She concludes with the rest of the information supplied by the
Iveses to whose letter she refers:

> In a letter to Miss Carabo, the composer has the following
> to say about this work. "The sonata in a way suggests, or
> at least tries to suggest, some of the outdoor life, the coun-
> try meetings, and the deep thoughts and feelings in many
> of those bygone days. The first and third movements
> would suggest some of the serious and religious part of
> those lives and the second movement would like to suggest
> the Farmers' Barn Dance of a Winter Night."

Her description provides as clear a listener's guide as one could wish for a first hearing and voices the composer's own thoughts. Even with the historical and theoretical emphasis of today, an astonishing number of performers fail to take account of the structure of the music they perform; Carol's sensitivity to these matters was exceptional. Her love of teaching may have entered into the making of the program notes; she and Carabo-Cone gave at least three of the *Sonata*'s performances on college campuses: Smith, Hofstra, and Manhattan.

Carol herself was keenly aware of Ives's historical importance. Lawrence Morris recalls her thrill as she enthusiastically described to him and his wife the music she had newly discovered of this composer.[14] Jotted comments on her drafts abandoned for the printed program notes preserve her thoughts: "his innovations precede Stravinsky and Schoenberg; father of indigenous American music; the most experimental of our time." As Wiley Hitchcock describes Ives's music engagingly: the

> simple and complex, traditional and radical, conventional
> and experimental, homespun and rarefied, spiritual and
> slapstick . . . jostle each other in neighbourly fashion.[15]

This particular *Sonata*, however, is surprisingly short on dissonant harmony. While this may account for Ives labelling it for "soft-ears," Ives pianist and scholar John Kirkpatrick observed, "Ives's genius made this triadic idiom just as fresh and strong as any experiment."[16] Given the mood in America, the triadic idiom and the familiar hymn tunes undoubtedly added to the appeal, making a difficult composer more accessible.

* * *

The manifestation of American nationalism indicated by the discovery of Ives and his music took other forms during the 'forties. In the expectations of a distinctly American music, critics prodded and chided; quite a number of composers delivered. Roy Harris (1898-1979) stands out among the deliverers. His supreme self-confidence and his deliberate use, some might insist, his exploitation of American materials (inevitably supplemented with stories of his own birth on Lincoln's birthday in an Oklahoma log cabin and his farm-boy upbringing) made him the "white hope of the nationalists," as John Tasker Howard labelled him in *Our American Music*.[17] He waxed, if not eloquent, at least prolific on the subject of America and her possibilities for native music:

> Wonderful, young, sinewy, timorous, browbeaten, eager,
> gullible American society, living in a land of grandeur,
> dignity, and untold beauty, is slowly kneading consistent
> racial character from the sifted flour of experience and the
> sweat of racial destiny [!]

reads one sentence from 1933.[18] Hundreds of others followed, so many, in fact, that Virgil Thomson eventually spluttered: "One would think, to read his prefaces, that he had been awarded by God, or at least by popular vote, a monopolistic privilege of expressing our nation's deepest ideals and highest aspirations."[19] Harris's spoken words offended no less than his written ones. He outraged many listeners on a radio interview in 1927 when he suddenly turned on his friendly interviewer, Olin Downes, to accuse the critic of believing that "all American composers of two generations lacked virility and other undesirable qualities."[20]

Self-appointed, strident, single-minded, Harris nevertheless thrived, and his music gained performance. Koussevitzky placed his *Third Symphony* on the opening concert of the Boston Symphony's New York season, November 23, 1939, "the first time that a leading orchestra of the country had devoted two of its subscription concerts exclusively to symphonic works by native composers."[21] In reviewing the concert, Olin Downes put his critical finger on the paradox of Harris's Americanism:

> The opening is striking in the breadth, the fashioning, and
> the spacious intervals of the main theme, not in itself
> distinguished or fascinating but projected with a fine stark-
> ness, yet suppleness of line, against a meager tonal back-
> ground. Some might say that the heroic bare hills and
> plains of parts of America could have inspired that. Others
> might discover in it more direct relationship to plainchant,
> of which Mr. Harris has made an earnest study in recent
> years.[22]

Harris, whose life on the California farm turns out to have been curiously close to bustling Los Angeles, broadened his alleged provincial horizons further with a sojourn in France as a reluctant pupil of Nadia Boulanger.[23] If he outwardly resisted her continental wisdom, he inwardly accepted her introduction to Medieval and Renaissance Europeans. Downes, whose own self-education ranged impressively wide, quickly perceived the futility of attributing parallel fifths and octaves to American primitivism rather than Medieval organum in such a composer.

Carol Robinson, as curious and informed at sixty as she had been at twenty, knew of Harris's background. When she came to perform his *Violin Sonata* composed in 1942, her knowledge of the "facts," beginning with the birth on Lincoln's birthday in the Oklahoma log cabin through the study of "Orlandus, des Pres, Palestrina," shows up in her draft for the program notes. Perhaps Carol felt a personal tie with Harris's American experience. Not only had she lived many happy childhood years in Lincoln's home of Springfield, Illinois, but a treasured family photo pictures her uncle Eben White, eldest brother of her mother, standing Honor Guard in full dress uniform at Lincoln's tomb shortly after the assassination.

Robinson and Carabo-Cone may have chosen Harris's *Sonata* because of its distinction in winning the prestigious Coolidge Prize for Chamber Music.[24] In their first scheduled performance, however, the fall of 1946, they encountered an unexpected obstacle: the fourth movement, a *Toccata* mailed to them by Harris from Colorado Springs, was lost in the mail. They performed without it; they hardly spoiled the integrity of the work, for Mills Music had originally published the first three movements separately with the titles *Fantasy* (I), *Dance of Spring* (II), and *Melody* (III). Harris eventually composed a new fourth movement, which, performed independently of the others, concluded the Robinson and Carabo-Cone program April 29, 1948, New York, Times Hall.

The most obviously "American" movement of the four seems to be the second, where Harris uses a tune identified by Dan Stehman as *I'll Be True to My Love* as the theme.[25] The piano's rocking 6/8 figuration in the right hand with its supporting parallel drone fifths in the left set the stage for this tune, marked *dolce*, to sound forth on the violin. Proceeding variation-like, Harris next gives the theme to the piano, harmonizing with open chords and allowing the violin to weave 6/8 embellishments. So he continues, each thematic restatement ever more richly elaborating the tune through figuration and expanded harmonies until the violin's sonorous rendering in augmentation (two measures after rehearsal 20 in the score). The altered chords and harmonic parallelisms seen earlier in Robinson's own musical compositions are observed here expanded into a sonata-length work whose sweep, quotation, and composer mark it as distinctly "American."

The century's leading researcher of "folk" melodies, Béla Bartók, advocated the assimilation of native materials:

> What is the best way for a composer to reap the full
> benefits of his studies in peasant music? It is to assimilate
> the idiom of peasant music so completely that he is able to
> forget all about it and use it as his musical mother tongue
> . . . It is the character of peasant music, indescribable in
> words, that must find its way into our music. It must be
> pervaded by the very atmosphere of peasant culture.[26]

Harris, however, unashamedly enjoyed quotation, mining folk idiom in
ways as diverse as choral folk song settings, with a minimum of distortion
of the original, to the quotation and variation technique of the *Violin
Sonata* to a more technically ingenious *Folksong Symphony*. In 1948, the
composer created a *Mass* constructed "on prototypes of American folk-
songs." Olin Downes, who reviewed the première, defended the construction, but, perhaps still stung by Harris's public accusation, found little to
admire in the composer's realization. "The folk-song element was
predominant as a melodic ingredient in masses by the greatest composer[s]
of the later medieval period," Downes wrote. "The precedent is more
than sound. But we find Mr. Harris' poly—shall we make a vile
pun—phony by comparison with that of the ancient period."[27]

Harris couched his attraction for Americana in what one senses is
deliberately homely fashion: "I was brought up with simple folk attitudes
by my pioneer parents. Folk music was as natural to our way of life as
corn bread and sweet milk."[28] Better documented than Harris's childhood simplicity is his intensive study of American music at the Library of
Congress in preparing a choral anthology, *Singing through the Ages*.[29]
As much as his vaunted "humble origins," his encounter with the primary
sources in the mid-1930s and with performers and scholars (such as Alan
Lomax, Burl Ives, the Golden Gate Quartet) in the early 1940s gave
Harris the necessary tools for his most purposefully "American" works.

* * *

Of the three composers whose violin sonatas Carol Robinson
played in the 'forties—Henry Cowell, Roy Harris, and Charles Ives—only
Cowell (1897-1965) was a personal friend. Eleanor Anderson recalls
Robinson's visits with Henry and Sidney Cowell in their Harlem dwelling
during the couple's years in New York.[30] That friendship may have
reached back to the 'twenties when Robinson had given nearly a dozen
performances of the composer's *Aeolian Harp*.

Carol Robinson and Henry Cowell shared an ardency for the avant garde, a natural gift for teaching, and a fascination with movement to music. Where Robinson urged her pupils to dance Baroque fugues and contemporary keyboard works, Cowell invented "elastic form—to help dancers and choreographers obtain musical building blocks of just the right size for their movements."[31]   Where Robinson composed and played for Elizabeth Delza's dancing, Cowell crafted the *Sophie Delza Dance* set for Elizabeth's sister. Sophie Delza interpreted the composer's *Dances of Activity* for flute, percussion and piano at the Civic Repertory Theatre in New York December 10, 1933.[32]   And as Robinson was rehearsing Ives's *Third Sonata*, the seeds of the Cowells' book on Charles Ives were sown—by Carol's friend, Gorham Munson, and Henry James.[33]   Mrs. Cowell recently recalled that Robinson's New York apartment served as the meeting place between Cowell and the prospective publishers as the book's idea took shape.[34]   Of Cowell's own music, Carol was an early enthusiast. Her performances of his *Aeolian Harp* in the 'twenties had brought substantial praise across the country. Thus, while the *Violin Sonata*, completed only in 1946, was new to Robinson, its composer was not.

In a curious way, the *Violin Sonata* bears a circuitous relationship to the *Aeolian Harp*. In 1930 or 1931 Cowell composed a melody for *How Old is Song?*, a poem his father had written.[35]   Soprano Judith Litante performed it in Town Hall, and Cowell played his *Aeolian Harp* as the harmonic background. Some years later when violinist Joseph Szigeti wanted Cowell to compose a sonata for him, the busy composer instead arranged *How Old is Song?* for violin, and the two of them performed this version, again accompanied with *Aeolian Harp*, at Carnegie Hall, March 11, 1944. Szigeti, however, wanted a larger work, one that exploited American folk fiddling, and eventually Cowell responded with the *Sonata for Violin and Piano*. He began as early as May 1945, but he did not complete the music until well into 1946, partly because Szigeti requested a fifth movement to be added to the original four.

Despite his crucial role in the *Sonata*'s creation, Szigeti, as it turned out, gave neither the first nor the second performance. Well before he finally played the piece with Joseph Levine in Carnegie Hall on February 6, 1949, audiences on both East and West coasts had heard Cowell's *Sonata*. On November 10, 1947, violinist Sol Babitz played it in Los Angeles with Cowell himself at the piano. Less than a year later, on April 29, 1948, Carol Robinson, with Carabo-Cone, gave the first New York performance in Times Hall.

No better contrast between the experimental mood of the 'twenties and the nationalistic one of the 'forties could be devised than the contrast between Cowell's *Aeolian Harp* and his *Violin Sonata.* Where the first strokes, plucks, and caresses the piano in new and unconventional ways, bypassing the keys to play directly on the strings, the second sounds forth on the piano's familiar keys in sturdy triadic harmonies and tuneful melodies. So old-fashioned did the work sound that the composer Vincent Persichetti described it as sounding like "an 18th-century colonial work written by a late 19th-century composer."[36]

Carol's thoughtful program notes explain the genesis of the work in terms that almost certainly came from Cowell himself, because they verbalize almost exactly Cowell's own explanations, printed later.[37] "Since 1941," she wrote,

> Cowell has been engaged on a series of compositions which are a modern development from the hymns and fuguing tunes of certain 18th-century American "primitive" composers. This superbly intense and sustained music did many things forbidden to 19th-century harmony.
>
> In 1941 when Cowell came across William Walker's "Southern Harmony"—a collection of shaped-note hymns in three parts, published in 1854—it recalled to him the music of primitive Baptists in Kansas, Oklahoma, and Iowa which he had heard on visits to relatives as a boy. When he realized how widespread and uninterrupted a rural folk tradition the "Southern Harmony" represented, he wondered what the result would have been if our musical culture had not cut itself off from its living roots, as it did during the last century—overawed by the achievements of Europe.
>
> The result of this inquiry has been a series of 12 pieces for various instrumental combinations, all under the title "Hymn and Fuging Tune." The Violin Sonata and his short symphony (no. 4) represent an elaboration of this American folk material. Both works begin with a hymn, and in addition to a fuguing tune, they each have incorporated the Irish-American ballad style in the slow movements with fiddle tunes for their scherzos.[38]

Carol reiterates what Cowell often said, though later writers have contradicted him: ` `"The tunes are original, not quotations." Then she explains her terms: `"A fuguing tune[39] differs from a fugue in having more than one theme at the original entry of the voices. Like all American folk music of Anglo-Saxon origin, it is likely to stick closer to the tonic of the original key than do European tunes."

"The third movement," she continues, "in song form, is in the 'Come-All-Ye' ballad style, and the fourth movement is a jig for the fiddle with a lively exchange of canonic imitations between the violin and piano" (her notes add her mental image: "who each seem to be trying to put the other off"). "The last movement is a summation, developing the material of the preceding movements" (described in her draft as a "broad and moving close—most elaborate.")

The traditions to which Cowell's *Sonata* pays allegiance stemmed from the eighteenth century and the so-called "first New England School" of American composers.[40] With energy, enthusiasm, and self-reliance, the Yankee tunesmiths, rejoicing in their freedom from conventional rules of composition, had crafted sturdy hymn tunes, rousing anthems, and canons. Their music, which possessed a rugged and powerful quality, was perhaps best exemplified by the works of that remarkable eighteenth-century individualist, William Billings.[41] Billings (1746-1800) had been a Boston tanner by trade, but in turning to the needs of the singing school and of composing, he became the first American to make music his sole profession. In the 1940s, Olin Downes, in his inimitable style, described William Billings thus to America's music lovers:

> An artisan, self-taught in music, a flaming vortex of religious and patriotic feeling, he was as independent as they make 'em. One-eyed, with a game leg and arms of unequal length, his appearance was as exceptional as his personality. His stentorian voice could bellow his music with deafening ardor. He broke the peace of a Boston meeting house with his "fuguing tunes" which he roundly declared to be "more than twenty times as beautiful as the old slow tunes," and cited their effect upon "the audiences, entertained and delighted, their minds surprisingly agitated and extremely fluctuated, sometimes declaring for one part and sometimes for another . . . Oh ecstatic! Rush on, you sons of harmony![42]

Billings's first tunebook, *The New-England Psalm-singer; or American Chorister*, published in 1770 with over 120 songs and a title page engraved by Paul Revere, bears all the earmarks of a swelling national consciousness. One of its hymns, *Chester*, became a rallying cry for the Revolution, its rebellious text penned by Billings himself, its music a marching song for the Minute Men from Maine to Georgia. "Let tyrants shake their iron rod," cried Billings,

> And slav'ry Clank her galling Chains

We fear them not we trust in god
New englands god for ever reigns.[43]

When *Chester* was reprinted in Billings's second tunebook, *The Singing Master's Assistant*, issued in fervently revolutionary Boston, 1778, Billings had added verses that named the enemy and that stridently described the enemy's transgressions.

Howe and Burgoyne and Clinton too,
With Prescot and Cornwallis join'd,
Together plot our Overthrow
In one Infernal league combin'd.

When God inspir'd us for the fight,
Their ranks were broke, their lines were forc'd,
Their Ships were Shatter'd in our sight,
Or swiftly driven from our Coast.

The Foe comes on with Haughty Stride,
Our troops advance with martial noise,
Their Vet'rans flee before our Youth,
And Gen'rals yield to beardless Boys.

What grateful Off'ring shall we bring,
What shall we render to the Lord,
Loud Hallelujahs let us Sing,
And praise his name on ev'ry Chord.[44]

The Singing Master's Assistant (a collection which came to be known as Billings's Best) also brought out the first fuging tunes to be composed by an American. Although not the inventor of fuging tunes, Billings figures large in their history. Fuging tunes, as Richard Crawford defines them, characteristically contain two sections; the first usually "... proceeds in block chords to a cadence. The second begins with overlapping contrapuntal entries, each voice singing the same text if not precisely the same subject; chordal texture is usually restored before the concluding cadence."[45] The fuging tune was thus not a fugue in the sense of a Bach fugue (hence, the modern spelling difference), although it did contain imitative passages. Presumably because of its contrapuntal delights, the fuging tune was beloved of eighteenth-century New Englanders. In describing their style, Wiley Hitchcock observed that the harmony (of these and other Yankee tunesmith works) was particularly distinctive, owing to the "open fifths, parallel fifths and octaves, modal inflections, and surprising dissonances . . ."[46]

The Cowell *Sonata*'s opening two movements exhibit these features so perfectly that one might well mistake this twentieth-century work for the creation of an earlier time. The first movement, entitled *Hymn* and marked *Largo* and "with fervor," boasts parallel octaves and fifths in the piano as well as sharply accented dissonances on unexpected beats. The fuging is separated here into a second movement, entitled *In Fuging Style*; with its angular theme, *fortissimo* dynamics, octave writing, and two-against-three rhythms, this imitative movement projects a crudely powerful vigor.

Yet, as Robinson had pointed out, Cowell's immediate predecessor and inspiration was not New England and the eighteenth-century tunesmiths but the South and its nineteenth-century heirs to the tunesmiths' tradition. Banished by increasingly sophisticated composers, such as Lowell Mason, the tunesmiths' repertory had migrated away from New England in the early nineteenth century and toward the south and west. In 1835 "Singin' Billy" Walker (1809-1875) of Spartanburg, South Carolina, published *The Southern Harmony*.[47] Popular lore has it that Walker compiled the book with his brother-in-law, Benjamin Franklin White, the men being married to sisters named Golightly. Yet on heading north to publish the volume, Walker took sole credit, thereby creating a family rift that never healed.[48] (Benjamin White, nevertheless, later produced his own eventually famous book, *The Sacred Harp*.) Within twenty years of its initial publication, *The Southern Harmony* had appeared in seven subsequent editions, and Walker boasted that more than 600,000 copies had been sold. The proud Walker began to add the initials, A.S.H. (author *Southern Harmony*) to his name (and supposedly those initials adorn his tombstone).[49] Containing more than 200 shape-note songs, *The Southern Harmony* includes works of Walker's own creation together with a rich array of fuging tunes, religious ballads, Yankee tunesmiths' music, refashioned Scottish and Irish music, and even *Hail, Columbia!* Tradition clearly ran strong and deep, if in geographical-ly erratic fashion.

Guided by the intermediary of *The Southern Harmony*, we can begin to appreciate that Cowell's *Violin Sonata* connects with multiple generations of America's music history. While Cowell revelled in the rugged sound of crude "American" harmonies in his first and second movements, the hymn and the fuging tune, in the third movement the composer turned to a wordless ballad, recalling the centuries-old practice of gathering the people together to hear a story (hence, the "come-all-ye" description[50]). For the fourth movement, Cowell composed a vivacious jig. If these third and fourth movements, the Ballad and Jig, call to mind

more Irish than American connections, there is not only the Irish element
in *The Southern Harmony* but also the diverse heritage of all immigrant
Americans on which to reflect. Cowell's own father came from Ireland
and on his mother's side, her relatives imbued him with a love of Irish
tunes. To be American virtually requires recognition of one's earlier
roots,[51] an awareness that enriches as it complicates the issue of an
American musical identity. Cowell managed to blend various elements of
American heritage in the *Violin Sonata*, synthesizing themes from all four
movements in the last, where he added the only whimsical use of the
piano in a coda.

* * *

Americans celebrating Americans—the theme resounds from each
Sonata and seemingly across America as individual actions gradually
swelled to an "American wave." Composers, self-conscious of their
Americanness, many fresh from the French fold of Boulanger, grew bold
in things American, especially as the Germans, formerly revered as
musical heroes, made political blunders across the twentieth century.
Performers—Ingolf Dahl and Sol Babitz, Carol Robinson and Carabo-
Cone, John Kirkpatrick, and Joseph Szigeti—sought out American music
old and new and began building an audience. Conductors and critics
advanced the same cause. One of the most enthusiastic promoters of
Americans was Serge Koussevitzky, whose all-American symphonic
programs appeared revolutionary. And together with those better known
as ardent lovers and avid collectors of American folk music—Alan and
John Lomax, Burl Ives, Ruth Crawford—the critic Olin Downes in
collaboration with Elie Siegmeister was compiling *A Treasury of American
Song* from the "multitudes and generations who have made America."
Including music from Billings to ballads, Downes evidently spoke for
many when he introduced *A Treasury*:

> If ever there was a time in the history of the nation that our
> people should know themselves and renew faith in the
> purposes and traditions which are part of us, that time is
> now.[52]

In the "now" of the 'thirties and 'forties, Americans in many aspects of
life proudly defined a national musical identity. Carol Robinson shows us
how, by the music she chose to perform and by the ideas she construed
as important. Through her we experience in a personal and specific way

the national artistic consciousness that engaged Americans in the aftermath of searing economic depression and world war.

* * *

Although she aged by the calendar, Carol Robinson remained youthful and vigorous, some would say imperious, in her outlook. Her nephew, who called her a "tough old bird," remembers ruefully the day she marched into the kitchen of an elegant New York restaurant, firmly demanding that his potatoes be served *hot*. But he also describes her admiringly as the youngest person he ever knew. In her late years when age and deteriorating health gradually curbed her activities, her lively curiosity continued unabated. Her papers contain articles explaining electronic music and Gagaku (the latter by her friend Faubion Bowers) as well as an early volume of *Perspectives of New Music* (I [1963]) with Pierre Boulez's article "Sonate, que me veux-tu?" liberally underlined. This volume appeared when Robinson was seventy-four years old, the same year that Marie Pierik published her *Dramatic and Symbolic Elements in Gregorian Chant*. Robinson's copy of Pierik's book contains underlinings (at centonization and *tonus peregrinus*) and black and white photos of Marie, perhaps taken at Brookhaven, pasted in front.

Carol's letters to Jean Réti-Forbes in the 'seventies speak of hearing Boulez conduct "beautiful" *Altenberg Lieder* and the incomparable Sviatoslav Richter playing Prokofiev ("On such another plane that I cannot describe it").[53] They also describe her own work: her teaching; "silent study of all the slow themes from the last 3 [Beethoven] string quartets (ties up with the slow movements of final 5 sonatas)"; and study of orchestration, "always . . . one of my passions."[54] In daily and sometimes excruciating pain, Robinson once told her nephew that while leaving off her blood pressure medicines could end her anguish and her life, her eagerness to see what each new day would bring deterred her from taking that irreversible step.[55] When she died at eighty-nine after nearly a decade of debilitating physical struggle, she had lived the better part of the twentieth century.

Given the present scholarly climate increasingly attuned to the contribution of women in all disciplines, we may legitimately view Carol Robinson in the light of feminist history. Among those confident individuals who set a course for others, Robinson never doubted her ability to be a valuable contributor to her chosen field. As have other women who did not know they were supposed to be inferior, Carol

Robinson seems to have assumed she could do anything and simply proceeded from there. Her attitude had its roots in her childhood of the 1890s, a time of significant reform for women, and in the fortunate examples of her mother, Clara White Robinson, and her teacher, Fannie Bloomfield Zeisler. Neither shaped by the often strident feminism of the 'seventies nor "burned out" earlier by the excesses of the 'twenties, Carol Robinson gives us an example of a woman who steadfastly maintained her personal right to pursue her own intellectual and artistic development and to function as an equal in the world.

However, Carol Robinson would almost certainly not have viewed her life in the context of feminism. While she did support and admire many feminists, from Margaret Anderson to H.D., she neither carried banners nor organized protest groups. As her niece related, Carol Robinson was a very practical woman in respect to this; she believed her talents were in music and the teaching of it, a vision established early in her life and reconfirmed in the Gurdjieff circles in which she moved. A woman who made lifelong learning a basic tenet of her personal philosophy, Robinson reached out to people and related to them as a teacher, tirelessly encouraging each individual's human awareness and self expression at every level. She herself made no distinctions of sex or other prejudice in her personal relations. She once sharply chastised her nephew for making a comment that she felt to be derogatory to Jews (among whom she counted some of her best friends and pupils). On another occasion she took one rather macho cousin completely aback when, taking his hand in her strong fingers, she asked if he had ever thought about playing the piano. Through some personal magic, Carol Robinson made those who knew her reach and soar higher than they had believed possible, if only for a little while.

Even now, something of Carol Robinson's magic seems to reach across time and space. Over the last two years, as her story has grown from an obscure name to nearer its present form, teaching and library faculty, students, neighbors, and friends have expressed repeated and lively interest in Carol Robinson's life; lectures including presentations of music, both from her collection and by her have generated immediate response;[56] and an ever-swelling host of her friends, students, and acquaintances has materialized to affirm her worth. Robinson intrigues us partly because she represents the many men as well as women whom historians have unjustifiably chosen to ignore while canonizing others. In Robinson's particular case, no one suspected that from a jumble of programs, newspaper clippings, unrelated books and articles, and music belonging to a person nowhere mentioned in a music history book there would emerge an enthralling musical life—much less, strange and wonderful vistas of the twentieth century. Robinson fascinates us too because her story effectively demonstrates that there are no mutually independent contemporaries; the wholeness of twentieth-century musical life that she helps us to see rings true with most of our own experiences. And then there are the personal details that Carol Robinson gives recent history which make her story so appealing and so valuable: hers was a life that expressively demonstrates the importance of individual commitment and one that provides human contact with a century fast slipping away.

In 1926 an Oregon reviewer commented after a Robinson recital: "It is fitting that the work of the moderns should be presented by one who is so distinctly modern herself."[57] Half a century later, Robinson appeared modern still as she sought those roads least travelled. For those of us journeying on toward the twenty-first century, Carol Robinson, at times inconspicuous, but as it turns out, not ever insignificant, provides an inspiring—and a sobering—model.

NOTES

1. Charles E. Ives, *Memos*, ed. John Kirkpatrick (New York: Norton, 1972), pp. 70, 71.

2. Ibid., p. 118.

3. Ibid., pp. 69-71, 118.

4. Ibid., pp. 70, 71.

5. *Music in the United States: A Historical Introduction*, 3d ed. (Englewood Cliffs, N.J.: Prentice-Hall, 1988), p. 219.

6. Ibid., p. 220.

7. *New York Herald Tribune*, 12 November 1946, p. 21.

8. GU MS 912, Correspondence "Rho-She," LS Carol, Robinson 16 June 1970. Robinson concludes this complaint with the only allusion to Gurdjieff that I have found among all of her papers: "these things have long since given me no negative thought (Gurdjieff possibly?)."

9.   Frank R. Rossiter, *Charles Ives and His America* (New York: Liveright, 1975), pp. 256ff.

10.   Ibid., p. 236. Robinson's copy, GU MS 300, Music Folder, is the revised *Third Sonata*, which according to Mrs. Ives was made in 1914. It agrees with the Yale University School of Music Library's *Whole Sonata* that John Kirkpatrick describes in "A Temporary Mimeographed Catalogue of the Music Manuscripts and related materials of Charles Edward Ives 1874-1954" (Yale University: 1960), pp. 80-81. The *Sonata* appeared in print in 1951, published by Merion Music, Inc., and highly edited by the performers Sol Babitz and Ingolf Dahl.

11.   Letter draft from Harmony Ives to Carabo-Cone, New Haven, Yale School of Music Library, Charles Ives Materials. A typed summary of Mrs. Ives's letter dated simply 15 October in MS 300, Box 3, Folder 3 reads like the Yale Library draft except for omitted pleasantries.

12.   So reads the unsigned summary of Mrs. Ives's letter in GU MS 300, Box 3, Folder 3.

13.   Ibid. The same folder also contains Robinson's drafts for her program notes.

14.   LS Lawrence Morris to the author, 12 December 1988.

15.   H. Wiley Hitchcock, *Ives*, Oxford Studies of Composers, no. 14 (London: Oxford University Press, 1977), p. 6.

16.   *Memos*, p. 71, nt. 7. Kirkpatrick suggests that the composer's dissatisfaction might have been with the metrical notation.

17.   John Tasker Howard, *Our American Music*, 3d ed., revised (New York: Thomas Y. Crowell Company, 1954), p. 456.

18.   Roy Harris, "Problems of American Composers," printed in *The American Composer Speaks*, ed. Gilbert Chase ([s.p.]: Louisiana State University Press, 1966), p. 148.

19.   *New York Herald Tribune*, 21 November 1940, p. 31.

20.   GU MS 688, Correspondence File, re: Harris, Roy, contains several exasperated letters from listeners referring to the incident.

21. *Olin Downes on Music. A Selection from His Writings during the Half-Century 1906 to 1955*, ed. Irene Downes (New York: Simon and Schuster, 1957), p. 280.

22. Ibid., p. 282.

23. Dan Stehman, in his biography *Roy Harris: An American Musical Pioneer* (Boston: Twayne Publishers, 1984), describes the teacher-pupil relationship, pp. 17-20.

24. CC Jane Meuer, 21 October 1946, GU MS 300, Box 3, Folder 3; apparently an agent for the performers, Meuer writes a form letter that emphasizes the Coolidge Prize and then goes on to explain how the fourth movement was lost. Her communication may be the source for the same story found in several clippings in MS 300, Box 1, Folder 10, including one identified and dated: the *New Hampshire Gazette*, 1 November 1946.

25. Stehman identifies the borrowed tune and discusses the *Sonata* in *Roy Harris*, pp. 210-215. Harris's source for this tune remains unclear. Belwin-Mills published the *Sonata* in a revised edition in 1974. The Publisher's Note that precedes the music reads: "We take great pride in presenting the definitive version of the Roy Harris Sonata for Violin and Piano. This final revision represents his thoughts on this work after more than thirty years of performance and reflection."

26. Quoted in *Music in the Western World, A History in Documents*, selected and annotated by Piero Weiss and Richard Taruskin (New York: Schirmer Books, 1984), p. 446.

27. *The New York Times*, 14 May 1948, clipping in GU MS 688, Subject File, Harris, Roy.

28. Quoted in Stehman, *Roy Harris*, p. 72.

29. By Roy Harris and Jacob Evanson (New York: American Book Co., 1940). On Harris's study in the Library of Congress, see Stehman, *Roy Harris*, pp. 72ff.

30. Interview with Eleanor Anderson, New York, 5 December 1988.

31.   William Lichtenwanger, *The Music of Henry Cowell, A Descriptive Catalogue*, I.S.A.M. monographs, no. 23 (Brooklyn, N.Y.: Institute for Studies in American Music, 1986), p. xiv.

32.   Ibid., pp. 39, 186.

33.   Henry Cowell and Sidney Cowell, *Charles Ives and His Music* (New York: Oxford University Press, 1955), p. vii.

34.   Telephone interview with Sidney Cowell, 16 April 1989.

35.   Lichtenwanger, *The Music of Henry Cowell*, pp. 94, 131-132, 219, provides the dates and performers that follow.

36.   Vincent Persichetti, "Reviews of Records: Modern American Music Series," *Musical Quarterly* 40 (1954): 475.

37.   Cowell's notes appeared on the record jacket of Joseph Szigeti and Carlo Bussoti's recording of the *Violin Sonata*, Columbia ML 4841 (1954).

38.   GU MS 300, Box 3, Folder 3 contains Robinson's notes.

39.   Today scholars have adopted the spelling "fuging" to diffentiate the process from that of a fugue.

40.   Two excellent starting points for the eighteenth-century tunesmiths and their nineteenth-century heirs and the sources on which the present account is based are Wiley Hitchcock's *Music in the United States,* chaps. 1 and 5; and Gilbert Chase, *America's Music from the Pilgrims to the Present*, revised 3d ed., with a Foreword by Richard Crawford (Urbana: University of Illinois Press, 1987), chap. 7.

41.   *William Billings of Boston, Eighteenth-century Composer*, by David P. McKay and Richard Crawford (Princeton: Princeton University Press, 1975), contains extensive biographical material and detailed musical information about Billings's tunebooks.

42.   *A Treasury of American Song*, text by Olin Downes and Elie Siegmeister; music arranged by Elie Siegmeister, 2d ed., revised and enlarged with a new Introduction (New York: Alfred A. Knopf, 1943), p. 49.

43. Quoted in McKay and Crawford, *William Billings*, p. 63. The
     tune, marked "at a rousing clip" and bearing Elie Siegmeister's
     harmonization, appears in Downes and Siegmeister's *A Treasury
     of American Song*, p. 62.

44. Quoted in McKay and Crawford, *William Billings*, pp. 63-64.

45. Richard Crawford, "Fuging-tune," in *The New Grove Dictionary
     of Music and Musicians*, 7: 9.

46. Hitchcock, *Music in the United States*, p. 17.

47. William Walker, *The Southern Harmony & Musical Companion*,
     ed. Glenn C. Wilcox (Lexington, Ky.: The University Press of
     Kentucky, 1987). This edition is a reproduction of a 1966 Pro
     Musicamericana reprint, which was itself printed from the 1854
     original.

48. Ibid., p. iii.

49. According to Wallace White, "A Reporter at Large; The Big
     Singing," *The New Yorker*, 19 January 1987, pp. 78-87. White
     reports the continuing popularity of *The Southern Harmony* with
     present-day singing groups.

50. Professor Lafayette Todd, of Hamilton College, Clinton, N.J.,
     described to the author how, in the 1930s, the Okies and Arkies
     still practiced this ballad style, kept alive through oral tradition.
     As a notated example, see "The Boston Come-All-Ye" in *A
     Treasury of American Song*, p. 92, which begins "Come all ye
     young sailor men, listen to me..."

51. Alan Levy, *Musical Nationalism. American Composers' Search
     for Identity* (Westport, Connecticut: Greenwood Press, 1983), pp.
     98-99.

52. *A Treasury of American Song*, p. 11.

53. LS 3 February 1920 and undated letter, both in GU MS 912,
     Correspondence "Rho-She." Robinson often writes of "wonderful
     radio," but friends note that she was careful to select only live
     performances. Millie Steinberg recalls her dismay when, after
     giving Robinson a favorite recording, she realized later that her
     teacher owned no record player.

54.   Ibid., LS 22 June 1971 and LS 7 September 1971.

55.   LS David Robinson to the author, 23 January 1989.

56.   These presentations include a paper read to the American Musico-
       logical Society's Capitol Chapter, Washington, D.C., 27 January
       1989; a lecture-demonstration for the Porter Kellam Conference,
       University of Georgia, Athens, Georgia, 9 May 1989; and a
       Lecture-Recital, University of Georgia, 18 May 1989.

57.   Flyer of Press Comments, GU MS 300, Box 1, Folder 2 (attribut-
       ed to the *Capitol-Journal*, Salem, Oregon, 30 March 1926).

W.E. Robinson, Carol Robinson's father.

Clara White Robinson, Carol Robinson's mother.

Carol Robinson, above, 1889; below, Clara White Robinson (left) the morning of a concert, June 1882.

The Robinson children, Ward, Carol, Clara, and Paul, in 1897.

Carol Robinson at High School graduation, c. 1906.

Early professional photograph of Carol Robinson, Chicago, c. 1916.

Carol Robinson in her Chicago studio, 1921.

Carol Robinson in 1925. Photograph by Marcia Stein, New York.

Margaret Anderson, above, and Jane Heap. Reproduced from *The Little Review*, Winter 1922 and May 1929.

Georgette Leblanc, above, and Pavel Tchelichev. Reproduced from *The Little Review*, May 1929 and Spring 1925.

Elinor Wylie. Photograph by Nickolas Muray, 1926. Yale Collection of American Literature, Beinecke Rare Book and Manuscript Library, Yale University. Reproduced by permission.

H.D. Photograph by Man Ray. Yale Collection of American Literature, Beinecke Rare Book and Manuscript Library, Yale University. Reproduced by permission of the Beinecke Library and the Man Ray Trust. © 1993 ARS, New York / ADAGP / The Man Ray Trust, Paris.

George Antheil. Reproduced from *The Little Review*, Spring 1925.

Bohuslav Martinů in Paris. From *Martinů* by Brian Large (New York: Holmes & Meier Publishers, Inc., 1975). Copyright © 1975 by Brian Large. Reproduced by permission of the publisher.

Elizabeth Delza dances Couperin.

Elizabeth Delza dances from *The Book of Job*; after drawings by William Blake to music of Sir Hubert Parry. Photograph by Soichi Sunami, New York.

APPENDIX A

CAROL ROBINSON'S PERFORMING REPERTORY

The following list together with dates and places of Robinson's performances has been compiled from programs and reviews in GU MS 300, the Carol Robinson collection. An asterisk indicates ensemble playing. Accompaniment on student recitals at Dalcroze is omitted. Where possible, opus numbers or other clarifying information have been added to the programs' citations in brackets.

ALALEONA, DOMINICO (1881-1928)

Italian Song [arrangement of 16th-century song, from *Canzoni italiane?*]

3/20/24	Williamstown, Mass.
10/26/24	Chicago, Playhouse
1/20/25	Springfield, Ill.
2/15/25	New York, Civic Club
2/26/25	Athol, Mass.
3/05/25	Newburyport, Mass., Music Club
3/20/25	Boston, Mass.
12/09/28	Paris, Students' Atelier Reunion

ALBÉNIZ, ISAAC (1860-1909)

Córdova [probably *Córdoba* from *Cantos de España*, Op. 232, 1896]

10/11/33	Rosemont, Pa., Rosemont College
3/20/47	Bronxville, N.Y., Women's College

ANTHEIL, GEORGE (1900-1959)

*Ballet mécanique

4/10/27	New York, Carnegie Hall

113

Jazz Sonata [Piano Sonata no. 4]

>   11/16/24   New York, Anderson Galleries, League of Compos-
>   ers First Lecture Recital. The *Jazz Sonata*, called
>   a "world première," was followed by Olin Downes's
>   lecture, "The Younger Generation in Music."
>   4/18/26   Portland, Ore., Pro-Musica Concert

AURIC, GEORGES (1899-1983)

Sonatine [in G, 1922] i. *Allegro*, ii. *Andante*, iii. *Presto*

>   12/18/23   Boston, Boston University
>   3/04/24   Boston, "First Boston performance"
>   10/26/24   Chicago, Playhouse
>   4/18/26   Portland, Ore., Pro-Musica Concert

BACH, CARL PHILIP EMMANUEL (1714-1788)

Allegro di molto [attributed to "Th. Emmanuel Bach"]

>   10/21/36   Rosemont, Pa.

Andante, from Clavichord Sonata in D minor [attributed simply to "Bach"]

>   3/20/47   Bronxvi'le, N.Y., Women's Club
>   6/08/47   San Antonio, Our Lady of the Lake College

Andante, from Clavichord Sonata no. 4 [same as above?]

>   7/25/40   Centerville, Mass.

BACH, JOHANN SEBASTIAN (1685-1750)

Adagio, A minor

>   10/18/34   Rosemont, Pa., Rosemont College

Bourrée, B minor

      10/18/34   Rosemont, Pa., Rosemont College

*Concerto in A minor for piano [*sic*], flute, violin [probably BWV 1044]

      12/06/53   Northampton, Mass., Smith College

Gigue from Partita in B-flat [BWV 825?]

      2/15/25   New York, Civic Club
      2/26/25   Athol, Mass.
      3/05/25   Newburyport, Mass., Music Club
      3/20/25   Boston
      3/21/26   San Antonio, Our Lady of the Lake College
      6/27/26   San Antonio, Our Lady of the Lake College
      7/12/34   Rosemont, Pa., Rosemont College

*Organ Chorale Prelude *In dir ist Freude* [BWV 615] (arr. Vivian Langrish) [for two pianos; published Schirmer]

      8/08/40   Centerville, Mass.
      4/05/57   New York, Dalcroze School, Faculty Recital

Organ Prelude in E minor

      12/11/38   Suffern, N.Y.

*Organ Prelude and Fugue in C major (arr. Ralph Lawton) [for two pianos], first performance, with Ralph Lawton

      8/08/40   Centerville, Mass.

Schafe können sicher weiden, Recitative and Aria from the Birthday Cantata [BWV 208] (arr. Mary Howe) [for two pianos; published Schirmer]

      8/08/40   Centerville, Mass.

Sicilienne from Sonata in E-flat for Piano and Flute [BWV 1031] (arr. Guy Maier) [for two pianos]

      8/08/40   Centerville, Mass.

Sonata for Flute and Piano, E-flat minor [*sic*]; [thus reported in *Dalcroze Bulletin*; presumably Sonata in E-flat major, BWV 1031]

        12/11/55   New York

BACH, WILHELM FRIEDEMANN (1710-1784)

Adagio

        12/10/29   Emmitsburg, Md.
        4/08/30   Springfield, Ill.

Largo

        11/01/29   Albany, N.Y., Women's Club

BACH-BAUER

Toccata, G major

        10/14/25   Mt. Carroll, Ill.
        10/21/25   Decatur, Ill.
        6/27/26   San Antonio, Our Lady of the Lake College
        7/10 or   Oldenburg, Ind., Convent of Our Sisters of
        7/11/26   St. Francis
        10/18/34   Rosemont, Pa., Rosemont College

Toccata, G minor

        10/19/25   Springfield, Ill.
        1/28/26   Millbrook, N.Y., Bennett School

Toccata [no key]

        3/15/26   Aurora, Ill.
        3/17/26   Lawrence, Kan., University of Kansas
        3/21/26   San Antonio, Our Lady of the Lake College
        3/29/26   Salem, Ore., Civic Music Club
        3/31/26   Portland, Ore.
        4/05/26   Seattle, Wash., Women's Century Club
        4/13/26   Medford, Ore., Andrews Conservatory

4/25/26	Pullman, Wash., State College of Washington
9/19/26	Woodstock, N.Y., Maverick Sunday Concerts
10/11/33	Rosemont, Pa., Rosemont College
1/17/?	New York, Fifth Avenue Playhouse

BACH-BUSONI

Choral, *Ich ruf' zu dir*

4/04/30	Warsaw, Ind., Zerelda Reading Club
4/06/30	Aurora, Ill.
11/17/30	St. Joseph, Mo., Fortnightly Music Club
11/18/30	St. Louis, Progressive Series Teachers College

BACH-LISZT

Fantasie, G minor [BWV 542]

12/30/28	Paris, Students and Artists' Club
3/10/29	Paris, American Women's Club
12/14/38	New York, St. Walburga's Academy

Fantasie and Fugue, G minor

10/18/34	Rosemont, Pa., Rosemont College

BACH-SAINT-SAËNS

Bourrée (B minor)

2/22/23	Chicago, Fortnightly Music Club
2/14/38	New York, St. Walburga's Academy

Gavote [*sic*]

Between 1/29 and 2/3/23	Chicago

BACH-SILOTI

Prelude, E minor

    2/14/38   New York, St. Walburga's Academy

BALAKIREV, MILY (1837-1910)

Scherzo [no. 1], B minor [1856]

1/03/22	Rogers Park, Ill., Women's Club
4/27/22	Decatur, Ill., Federation of Music Clubs
2/27/24	Boston, MacDowell Club
3/20/24	Williamstown, Mass.
3/21/24	Worchester, Mass., Mechanics Hall
2/15/25	New York, Civic Club
2/26/25	Athol, Mass.
3/20/25	Boston
3/21/26	San Antonio, Our Lady of the Lake College
3/29/26	Salem, Ore., Civic Music Club
3/31/26	Portland, Ore.
4/05/26	Seattle, Wash., Women's Century Club
4/13/26	Medford, Ore., Andrews Conservatory
6/16/26	San Antonio, Incarnate Word College
6/27/26	San Antonio, Our Lady of the Lake College
7/10 or	Oldenburg, Ind., Convent of the Sisters of
7/11/26	St. Francis
11/03/26	New York, Studio Guild and WOR
10/21/36	Rosemont, Pa., Rosemont College

BARTÓK, BÉLA (1881-1945)

Dirge, Op. 8, no. 2

    7/25/40   Centerville, Mass.

Élégie [Op. 8b *Ket elegia* (Two elegies, 1908, 1909)]

5/23/29	New York, Afternoon musicales
4/08/30	Springfield, Ill.
11/17/30	St. Joseph, Mo., Fortnightly Music Club

11/18/30	St. Louis, Progressive Series Teachers College
10/18/34	Rosemont, Pa., Rosemont College
1/28/36	Millbrook, N.Y., Bennett School
4/05/42	Northampton, Mass., Smith College [Marked "Op. 8b, no. 1"]
6/08/47	San Antonio, Our Lady of the Lake College

BEECHER, CARL MILTON (1883-1968)

Waltz (also *Valse*) in B [or B-flat] minor, dedicated to Carol Robinson

2/26/21	Chicago, Leon Mandel Hall
2/15/25	New York, Civic Club
3/20/25	Boston, Steinert Hall [Program specifies that the waltz is "dedicated to Miss Robinson"]
6/26/25	St. Louis, Progressive Series Teachers College
7/07/27	New York, New York University
8/31/27	Oldenburg, Ind., Convent of the Sisters of St. Francis
9/01/27	Oldenburg, Ind., Convent of the Sisters of St. Francis
3/05/28	New York, Columbia University
12/09/28	Paris, Students' Atelier
5/23/29	New York, Afternoon musicales

BEETHOVEN, LUDWIG VAN (1770-1827)

Op. 13 [Sonata no. 8, C minor, Pathétique]

10/26/24	Chicago, Playhouse
1/20/25	Springfield, Ill.
2/26/25	Athol, Mass.
3/05/25	Newburyport, Mass., Music Club
6/18/25	St. Louis, Progressive Series Teachers College
7/12/25	San Antonio, Our Lady of the Lake College
3/17/26	Lawrence, Kan., University of Kansas
3/29/26	Salem, Ore., Civic Music Club
3/31/26	Portland, Ore.
4/13/26	Medford, Ore., Andrews Conservatory

Op. 27, no. 2 [Sonata no. 14 'quasi una fantasia', C-sharp minor]

4/04/30	Warsaw, Ind., Zerelda Reading Club
4/06/30	Aurora, Ill.
11/17/30	St. Joseph, Mo., Fortnightly Music Club
10/11/33	Rosemont, Pa., Rosemont College [program actually reads Op. 22, no. 2]

Op. 31, no. 3 [Sonata no. 18, E-flat major]

10/21/36	Rosemont, Pa., Rosemont College

Op. 90 [Sonata no. 27, E minor]

3/20/25	Boston
10/14/25	Mt. Carroll, Ill.
10/19/25	Springfield, Ill.
10/21/25	Decatur, Ill.
1/28/26	Millbrook, N.Y., Bennett School
3/15/26	Aurora, Ill.
3/21/26	San Antonio, Our Lady of the Lake College
1/24/36	Millbrook, N.Y., Bennett School
4/05/42	Northampton, Mass., Smith College

*Piano Trio, Op. 1, no. 3 [C minor]

3/22/57	New York, Dalcroze Faculty Recital

BORODIN, ALEXANDER (1833-1887)

Au convent ["In the Monastery" from *Petite suite*]

4/27/22	Decatur, Ill., Federation of Music Clubs
3/20/24	Williamstown, Mass.
3/21/24	Worcester, Mass., Mechanics Hall
10/26/24	Chicago, Playhouse

BORTKIEWICZ, SERGEI (1877-1952)

Etude, C-sharp major [probably from Ten Etudes, Op. 15]

1/03/22	Rogers Park, Ill., Women's Club
6/26/25	St. Louis, Progressive Series Teachers College
12/10/29	Emmitsburg, Md.

Etude, C-sharp minor

2/15/25	New York, Civic Club
2/26/25	Athol, Mass.
3/20/25	Boston
5/23/29	New York, Afternoon musicales

Etude, F-sharp minor

3/20/24	Williamstown, Mass.
3/21/24	Worcester, Mass.
2/15/25	New York, Civic Club
2/26/25	Athol, Mass.
3/05/25	Newburyport, Mass., Music Club
3/20/25	Boston
6/26/25	St. Louis, Progressive Series Teachers College
2/24/27	Boston, MacDowell Club
12/09/28	Paris, Students' Atelier
5/23/29	New York, Afternoon musicales
12/10/29	Emmitsburg, Md.
7/12/34	Rosemont, Pa., Rosemont College

BRAHMS, JOHANNES (1833-1897)

Ballade, Op. 10, no. 1 [D minor, "Edward," 1854]

10/21/36	Rosemont, Pa., Rosemont College
12/11/55	New York, Museum of the City of N.Y.

Capriccio, Op. 76, no. 2 [B minor, 1878]

2/26/20	Highland Park, Ill.
12/30/28	Paris, Students and Artists' Club
1/24/36	Millbrook, N.Y., Bennett School
3/20/47	Bronxville, N.Y., Women's Club
6/08/47	San Antonio, Our Lady of the Lake College
12/11/55	New York, Museum of the City of N.Y.

Intermezzo, Op. 118, no. 2 [A major, 1892]

7/12/34	Rosemont, Pa., Rosemont College
10/18/34	Rosemont, Pa., Rosemont College

Rhapsody, Op. 119, no. 4 [E-flat major, 1892]

10/14/25	Mt. Carroll, Ill.
10/19/25	Springfield, Ill.
10/21/25	Decatur, Ill.
1/28/26	Millbrook, N.Y., Bennett School
3/15/26	Aurora, Ill.
3/17/26	Lawrence, Kan., University of Kansas
3/21/26	San Antonio, Our Lady of the Lake College
3/29/26	Salem, Ore., Civic Music Club
3/31/26	Portland, Ore.
4/05/26	Seattle, Wash., Women's Century Club
4/13/26	Medford, Ore., Andrews Conservatory
4/25/26	Pullman, Wash., State College of Washington
6/27/26	San Antonio, Our Lady of the Lake College
7/10 or	Oldenburg, Ind., Convent of the Sisters of
7/11/26	St. Francis
9/19/26	Woodstock, N.Y., Maverick Sunday Concerts
11/03/26	New York, Studio Guild and WOR
3/10/29	Paris, American Women's Club
11/01/29	Albany, N.Y., Women's Club
12/10/29	Emmitsburg, Md.
1/24/36	Millbrook, N.Y., Bennett School
1/17/?	New York, Fifth Avenue Playhouse

Rhapsody [no key nor opus number given]

6/16/26	San Antonio, Incarnate Word College

Romance, op. 118, no. 5 [F major, 1892]

2/26/20	Highland Park, Ill.
7/12/34	Rosemont, Pa., Rosemont College
12/11/38	Suffern, N.Y.
3/20/47	Bronxville, N.Y., Women's Club
6/08/47	San Antonio, Our Lady of the Lake College

Scherzo [Op. 4, E-flat minor, 1851]

>Between 1/29 and 2/3/23 Chicago [literally, the program reads "Scherzo, from Sonata, Op. 4"]

>10/11/33   Rosemont, Pa., Rosemont College

Sonata, Op. 5 [no. 3, F minor, 1853]

>12/11/38   Suffern, N.Y.
>3/22/39   Rosemont, Pa., Rosemont College
>4/04/39   Peoria, Ill.
>5/22/39   New York, St. Walburga's Academy
>7/25/40   Centerville, Mass.

*Violin Sonata no. 2 [Op. 100, A major, 1886]

>3/7/15   Chicago, Fine Arts Building, with Josephine Gerwig
>8/19/41   Long Island, for the benefit of the Red Cross, with Sigmund Michota

Waltzes [from Op. 39, 16 Waltzes]

>4/04/30   Warsaw, Ind., Zerelda Reading Club
>4/06/30   Aurora, Ill.
>4/08/30   Springfield, Ill.
>11/17/30   St. Joseph, Mo., Fortnightly Music Club
>11/18/30   St. Louis, Mo., Progressive Series Teachers College

Waltzes

>3/04/28 New York, Columbia University

BRIDGE, FRANK (1879-1941)

Fragrance [from *Four Characteristic Pieces*, 1915]

>Between 1/29-2/3/23 Chicago

CANTALLOS [(b. c. 1760), according to *The Spanish Harpsichordists*, ed. Giuliana Marchi (London: G. Ricordi, 1945)]

Sonata, C minor

10/21/36	Rosemont, Pa., Rosemont College
12/11/38	Suffern, N.Y.
4/04/39	Peoria, Ill.

CHABRIER, EMMANUEL (1841-1894)

Bourrée fantasque (1891)

4/27/22	Decatur, Ill., Federation of Music Clubs
2/26/25	Athol, Mass.
3/20/25	Boston
6/26/25	St. Louis, Progressive Series Teachers' College
7/12/25	San Antonio, Our Lady of the Lake College
7/17/25	San Antonio, Our Lady of the Lake College, Commencement Exercises
8/30/25	Glencoe, Ill.
10/14/25	Mt. Carroll, Ill.
10/19/25	Springfield, Ill.
10/21/25	Decatur, Ill.
1/28/26	Millbrook, N.Y., Bennett School
3/21/26	San Antonio, Our Lady of the Lake College
3/29/26	Salem, Ore., Civic Music Club
3/31/26	Portland, Ore.
4/05/26	Seattle, Wash., Women's Century Club
4/13/26	Medford, Ore., Andrews Conservatory
12/30/28	Paris, Students and Artists' Club
3/10/29	Paris, American Women's Club
5/23/29	New York, Afternoon musicales
7/12/34	Rosemont, Pa., Rosemont College
1/17/?	New York, Fifth Avenue Playhouse

CHOPIN, FRÉDÉRIC (1810-1849)

Ballade, Op. 38, F major

1/24/36	Millbrook, N.Y., Bennett School
2/14/38	New York, St. Walburga's Academy

12/11/38   Suffern, N.Y.
3/22/39   Rosemont, Pa., Rosemont College
4/04/39   Peoria, Ill.

Ballade, Op. 47 [A-flat major]

10/26/24   Chicago, Playhouse
1/20/25   Springfield, Ill.
2/26/25   Athol, Mass.
3/05/25   Newburyport, Mass., Music Club
5/15/27   ?, Douglaston Club
7/07/27   New York, New York University
8/31/27   Oldenburg, Ind., Convent of the Sisters of
             St. Francis
9/01/27   Oldenburg, Ind., Convent of the Sisters of
             St. Francis
3/20/47   Bronxville, N.Y., Women's Club
?   San Antonio, Our Lady of the Lake College

Ballade, Op. 48 [*sic*; Op. 48 is a set of Nocturnes; perhaps an error for Op. 38?]

3/20/25   Boston

Ballade

3/29/26   Salem, Ore., Civic Music Club

Barcarolle, Op. 60 [F-sharp major]

3/15/26   Aurora, Ill.
3/17/26   Lawrence, Kan., University of Kansas
3/21/26   San Antonio, Our Lady of the Lake College
3/29/26   Portland, Ore.
4/05/26   Seattle, Wash., Women's Century Club
4/13/26   Medford, Ore., Andrews Conservatory
4/25/26   Pullman, Wash., State College of Washington
11/01/29   Albany, N.Y., Women's Club
12/10/29   Emmitsburg, Md.
4/08/30   Springfield, Ill.
10/11/33   Rosemont, Pa., Rosemont College
10/21/36   Rosemont, Pa., Rosemont College
5/22/39   New York, St. Walburga's Academy

7/25/40	Centerville, Mass.
8/19/42	Long Island, Red Cross Benefit
12/11/55	New York, Museum of the City of N.Y.

Etude, Op. 10, no. 3 [E major]

2/26/21	Chicago, Leon Mandel Hall
6/18/25	St. Louis, Progressive Series Teachers College
6/16/26	San Antonio, Incarnate Word College
7/10 or	Oldenburg, Ind., Convent of the Sister of
7/11/26	St. Francis

Etude, Op. 10, no. 12 [C minor]

6/18/25	St. Louis, Progressive Series Teachers College

Etude, Op. 25, no. 8 [D-flat major]

6/18/25	St. Louis, Progressive Series Teachers College

Impromptu, Op. 36, F-sharp major

2/26/20	Highland Park, Ill.
10/26/24	Chicago, Playhouse
1/20/25	Springfield, Ill.
2/26/25	Athol, Mass.
6/18/25	St. Louis, Progressive Series Teachers College
7/12/25	San Antonio, Our Lady of the Lake College
6/16/26	San Antonio, Incarnate Word College
7/10 or	Oldenburg, Ind., Convent of the Sisters of
7/11/26	St. Francis
11/01/29	Albany, N.Y., Women's Club
1/24/36	Millbrook, N.Y., Bennett School
3/20/47	Bronxville, N.Y., Women's Club

Impromptu [no key nor opus given]

3/29/26	Salem, Ore., Civic Music Club

Mazurka, [no opus no.] A minor

3/22/39	Rosemont, Pa., Rosemont College
4/04/39	Peoria, Ill.

5/22/39   New York, St. Walburga's Academy
8/19/42   Long Island, Red Cross Benefit

Mazurka [no key nor opus given]

4/06/30   Aurora, Ill.
4/08/30   Springfield, Ill.

Nocturne, Op. 32, no. 1 [B major]

10/21/36   Rosemont, Pa., Rosemont College

Nocturne [Op. 37, no. 2] G major

2/26/20   Highland Park, Ill.
10/26/24   Chicago, Playhouse
6/18/25   St. Louis, Progressive Series Teachers' College
7/12/25   San Antonio, Our Lady of the Lake College
11/17/30   St. Joseph, Mo., Fortnightly Music Club
11/18/30   St. Louis, Progressive Series Teachers' College

Nocturne, Op. 48, no. 1, C minor

Between 1/29
and 2/3/23   Chicago
11/03/26   New York, Studio Guild and WOR
5/15/27   ?, Douglaston Club
7/07/27   New York, N.Y.U.
8/31/27   Oldenburg, Ind., Convent of the Sisters of
            St. Francis
9/01/27   Oldenburg, Ind., Convent of the Sisters of
            St. Francis
3/04/28   New York, Columbia University
3/10/29   Paris, American Women's Club
11/01/29   Albany, N.Y., Women's Club
12/10/29   Emmitsburg, Md.
1/24/36   Millbrook, N.Y., Bennett School
12/11/38   Suffern, N.Y.
6/08/47   San Antonio, Our Lady of the Lake College

Nocturne [no key nor opus no. given]

1/20/25   Springfield, Ill.

Polonaise, Op. 26, no. 1 [C-sharp minor]

3/20/25	Boston
6/18/25	St. Louis, Progressive Series Teachers College
3/29/26	Portland, Ore.
4/05/26	Seattle, Women's Century Club
4/14/26	Medford, Ore., Andrews Conservatory
6/16/26	San Antonio, Incarnate Word College
7/10 or	Oldenburg, Ind., Convent of the Sisters of
7/11/26	St. Francis

Prelude, Op. 28, no. 16 [B-flat minor]

6/18/25	St. Louis, Progressive Series Teachers College
7/12/25	San Antonio, Our Lady of the Lake College

Prelude, Op. 45, C-sharp minor

1/24/36	Millbrook, N.Y., Bennett School

Scherzo, [Op. 20] B minor

2/26/20	Highland Park, Ill.
2/26/21	Chicago, Leon Mandel Hall
4/27/22	Decatur, Ill., Federation of Music Clubs
12/18/23	Boston, Boston University
3/04/24	Boston, Steinert Hall
3/20/24	Williamstown, Mass.
8/30/25	Glencoe, Ill.
10/14/25	Mt. Carroll, Ill.
10/19/25	Springfield, Ill.
10/21/25	Decatur, Ill.
1/28/26	Millbrook, N.Y., Bennett School
6/16/26	San Antonio, Incarnate Word College
7/10 or	Oldenburg, Ind., Convent of the Sisters of
7/11/26	St. Francis
11/17/30	St. Joseph, Mo., Fortnightly Music Club
11/18/30	St. Louis, Progressive Series Teachers College
7/12/34	Rosemont, Pa., Rosemont College
10/18/34	Rosemont, Pa., Rosemont College

Scherzo, A minor [*sic*; the 4 Scherzi are in the keys of B, B-flat/D-flat, C-sharp, E]

1/07/24	Medford, Ore.
1/11/24	Salem, Ore.
1/15/24	Portland, Ore.
1/17/24	Seattle, Wash.

COUPERIN, FRANÇOIS (1668-1733)

Gentle Nanette [probably from *La Fleurie ou la tendre nanette*]

3/22/39   Rosemont, Pa., Rosemont College

Little Windmills [probably from *le 17e ordre*, E minor: *Les petits moulins à vent*]

3/22/39   Rosemont, Pa., Rosemont College

COWELL, HENRY (1897-1965)

Aeolian Harp (c. 1923) [for piano strings]

3/15/26	Aurora, Ill.
3/17/26	Lawrence, Kan., University of Kansas
3/21/26	San Antonio, Our Lady of the Lake College
3/31/26	Portland, Ore.
4/05/26	Seattle, Wash., Women's Century Club
4/13/26	Medford, Ore., Andrews Conservatory
4/25/26	Pullman, Wash., State College of Washington
6/16/26	San Antonio, Incarnate Word College
6/27/26	San Antonio, Our Lady of the Lake College

Sonata [for Violin and Piano; completed 1946]

4/29/48   New York [first New York performance and apparently second performance ever, preceded only by Sol Babitz in Los Angeles, 10 November 1947; although dedicated to Joseph Szigeti, Szigeti did not perform the work until 6 February 1949 with Joseph Levine in Carnegie Hall; see Lichtenwanger, *The Music of Henry Cowell*, p. 219].

DAQUIN, LOUIS-CLAUDE (1694-1772)

The Cuckoo

6/18/25	St. Louis, Progressive Series Teachers College
7/12/25	San Antonio, Our Lady of the Lake College
8/30/25	Glencoe, Ill.
10/14/25	Mt. Carroll, Ill.
10/19/25	Springfield, Ill.
10/21/25	Decatur, Ill.
1/28/26	Millbrook, N.Y., Bennett School
3/15/26	Aurora, Ill.
3/17/26	Lawrence, Kan., University of Kansas
3/29/26	Salem, Ore., Civic Music Club
3/31/26	Portland, Ore.
4/05/26	Seattle, Wash., Women's Century Club
4/13/26	Medford, Ore., Andrews Conservatory
4/25/26	Pullman, Wash., State College of Washington
6/16/26	San Antonio, Incarnate Word College
7/10 or	Oldenburg, Ind., Convent of the Sisters of
7/11/26	St. Francis
11/01/29	Albany, N.Y., Women's Club
7/25/40	Centerville, Mass.

DEBUSSY, CLAUDE (1862-1918)

Arabesque [presumably from *Deux Arabesques*, 1888-89]

7/10 or	Oldenburg, Ind., Convent of the Sisters of
7/11/26	St. Francis
3/22/39	Rosemont, Pa., Rosemont College

La Cathédrale engloutie [1910; from *Preludes*, Book I]

10/21/36	Rosemont, Pa., Rosemont College

Clair de Lune [from *Suite bergamasque*, 1890; revised 1905]

7/12/34	Rosemont, Pa., Rosemont College

Delphic Dancers [*Danseuses de Delphes*, 1909; from *Preludes*, Book I]

3/21/26	San Antonio, Our Lady of the Lake College
3/29/26	Salem, Ore., Civic Music Club
4/13/26	Medford, Ore., Andrews Conservatory
9/19/26	Woodstock, N.Y., Maverick Sunday Concerts
11/03/26	New York, Studio Guild and WOR
3/04/28	New York, Columbia University
5/23/29	New York, Afternoon musicales
11/01/29	Albany, N.Y., Women's Club
10/11/33	Rosemont, Pa., Rosemont College
8/19/42	Long Island, Red Cross Benefit

*En blanc et noir, no. 1 [1915; composed for two pianos]

8/08/40	Centerville, Mass.
4/05/57	New York, Dalcroze Faculty Recital

Jardins sous la pluie [from *Estampes*, 1903]

11/01/29	Albany, N.Y., Women's Club
12/10/29	Emmitsburg, Md.
4/04/30	Warsaw, Ind., Zerelda Reading Club
4/06/30	Aurora, Ill.
4/08/30	Springfield, Ill.
11/17/30	St. Joseph, Mo., Fortnightly Music Club
11/18/30	St. Louis, Progressive Series Teachers College
1/24/36	Millbrook, N.Y., Bennett School
5/22/39	New York, St. Walburga's Academy
3/20/47	Bronxville, N.Y., Women's Club
6/08/47	San Antonio, Our Lady of the Lake College

The Little Shepherd [from *Children's Corner*, 1906-08]

10/11/33	Rosemont, Pa., Rosemont College
8/19/42	Long Island, Red Cross Benefit

Poissons d'or [from *Images*, set 2, 1907]

10/21/36	Rosemont, Pa., Rosemont College
2/14/38	New York, St. Walburga's Academy

Valse "La plus que lente" [1910]

4/27/22	Decatur, Ill., Federation of Music Clubs
2/24/24	Boston, MacDowell Club
6/26/25	St. Louis, Progressive Series Teachers College
7/12/25	San Antonio, Our Lady of the Lake College
10/14/25	Mt. Carroll, Ill.
10/19/25	Springfield, Ill.
10/21/25	Decatur, Ill.
3/15/26	Aurora, Ill.
3/17/26	Lawrence, Kan., University of Kansas
3/29/26	Salem, Ore., Civic Music Club
4/25/26	Pullman, Wash., State College of Washington
7/10 or	Oldenburg, Ind., Convent of the Sisters of
7/11/26	St. Francis
3/10/29	Paris, American Women's Club
5/23/29	New York, Afternoon musicales
1/17/?	New York, Fifth Avenue Playhouse

DELIBES, LEO (1836-1891)

Passepied

3/20/24	Williamstown, Mass.
10/26/24	Chicago, Playhouse
1/20/25	Springfield, Ill.
2/15/25	New York, Civic Club
2/26/25	Athol, Mass.
3/05/25	Newburyport, Mass., Music Club

DOHNÁNYI, ERNŐ (1877-1960)

Rhapsody [Op. 11, no. 2, 1902-03] F-sharp minor

2/26/21	Chicago, Leon Mandel Hall
2/14/38	New York, St. Walburga's Academy

DE FALLA, MANUEL (1876-1946)

Andaluza [from *Pièces espagnoles*, 1902-08]

Between 1/29 and 2/3/23	Chicago
2/22/23	Chicago, Fortnightly Music Club
12/18/23	Boston, Boston University
1/07/24	Medford, Ore.
1/11/24	Salem, Ore.
1/15/24	Portland, Ore.
1/17/24	Seattle, Wash.
3/04/24	Boston, Steinert Hall
3/20/24	Williamstown, Mass.
3/21/24	Worcester, Mass., Mechanics Hall
1/20/25	Springfield, Ill.
2/15/25	New York, Civic Club
2/26/25	Athol, Mass.
3/05/25	Newburyport, Mass., Music Club
6/26/25	St. Louis, Progressive Series Teachers College
7/12/25	San Antonio, Our Lady of the Lake College
8/30/25	Glencoe, Ill.
3/15/26	Aurora, Ill.
3/17/26	Lawrence, Kan., University of Kansas
7/10 or 7/11/26	Oldenburg, Ind., Convent of the Sisters of St. Francis
9/19/26	Woodstock, N.Y., Maverick Sunday Concerts
5/23/29	New York, Afternoon musicales
11/01/29	Albany, N.Y., Women's Club
12/10/29	Emmitsburg, Md.
4/08/30	Springfield, Ill.
10/18/34	Rosemont, Pa., Rosemont College
1/24/36	Millbrook, N.Y., Bennett School
7/25/40	Centerville, Mass.
4/05/42	Northampton, Mass., Smith College
8/19/42	Long Island, Red Cross Benefit
3/20/47	Bronxville, N.Y., Women's Club
6/08/47	San Antonio, Our Lady of the Lake College

Ritual Fire Dance [*Danse Rituelle de Feu*, arranged from the ballet *El Amor Brujo*]

12/18/23	Millbrook, N.Y., Bennett School
1/07/24	Medford, Ore.
1/11/24	Salem, Ore.
1/15/24	Portland, Ore.
7/17/24	Seattle, Wash.
3/04/24	Boston, Steinert Hall
3/20/24	Williamstown, Mass.
3/21/24	Worcester, Mass., Mechanics Hall
10/26/24	Chicago, Playhouse; "by request"
1/20/25	Springfield, Ill.
2/15/25	New York, Civic Club
6/26/25	St. Louis, Progressive Series Teachers College
7/12/25	San Antonio, Our Lady of the Lake College, Commencement Exercises
8/30/25	Glencoe, Ill.
10/14/25	Mt. Carroll, Ill.
10/19/25	Springfield, Ill.
10/21/25	Decatur, Ill.
1/28/26	Millbrook, N.Y., Bennett School
3/15/26	Aurora, Ill.
3/17/26	Lawrence, Kan., University of Kansas
4/25/26	Pullman, Wash., State College of Washington
7/10 or	Oldenburg, Ind., Convent of the Sisters of
7/11/26	St. Francis
9/19/26	Woodstock, N.Y., Maverick Sunday Concerts
11/03/26	New York, Studio Guild and WOR
3/04/28	New York, Columbia University
12/09/28	Paris, Students' Atelier
5/23/29	New York, Afternoon musicales
11/01/29	Albany, Women's Club
1/17/?	New York, Fifth Avenue Playhouse

*Danse

4/23/?	New York, Anderson Galleries with Henri

FRANCK, CÉSAR (1822-1890)

Prelude and Choral

      7/12/34   Rosemont, Pa., Rosemont College

Prelude, Choral and Fugue [1884; see Wilhelm Mohr, *Caesar Franck*, 2d ed. (Tutzing, Hans Schneider, 1969), p. 230. This work is listed among the solo piano works. No separate Prelude and Choral are given.]

11/01/16	Chicago
11/20/16	New York, Comedy Theatre
12/18/23	Boston, Boston University
3/20/25	Boston
12/11/38	Suffern, N.Y.
3/22/39	Rosemont, Pa., Rosemont College
4/04/39	Peoria, Ill.
5/22/39	New York, St. Walburga's Academy
4/05/42	Northampton, Mass., Smith College

GLIÈRE, REINHOLD (1875-1956)

*Prelude, Chanson and Basso Ostinato, from Op. 41 [for 2 pianos, available Schirmer]

      4/05/57   New York, Dalcroze Faculty Recital

GLUCK-BRAHMS

Gavotte

6/18/25	St. Louis, Progressive Series Teachers College
7/12/25	San Antonio, Our Lady of the Lake College
8/30/25	Glencoe, Ill.
10/14/25	Mt. Carroll, Ill.
10/19/25	Springfield, Ill.
10/21/25	Decatur, Ill.
1/28/26	Millbrook, N.Y., Bennett School
3/15/26	Aurora, Ill.
3/17/26	Lawrence, Kan., University of Kansas
3/21/26	San Antonio, Our Lady of the Lake College

3/29/26	Salem, Ore., Civic Music Club
3/31/26	Portland, Ore.
4/05/26	Seattle, Wash., Women's Century Club
4/13/26	Medford, Ore., Andrews Conservatory
4/25/26	Pullman, Wash., State College of Washington
6/16/26	San Antonio, Incarnate Word College
7/10 or	Oldenburg, Ind., Convent of the Sisters of
7/11/26	St. Francis
3/04/28	New York, Columbia University
12/09/28	Paris, Students' Atelier
11/01/29	Albany, N.Y., Women's Club
12/10/29	Emmitsburg, Md.
4/04/30	Warsaw, Ind., Zerelda Reading Club
11/17/30	St. Joseph, Mo., Fortnightly Music Club
1/24/36	Millbrook, N.Y., Bennett School
12/11/38	Suffern, N.Y.
5/22/39	New York, St. Walburga's Academy
1/17/?	New York, Fifth Avenue Playhouse

GLUCK-CHASINS

*Melody, from *Orpheus* [*Orfeo ed Euridice*]

4/05/57	New York, Dalcroze Faculty Recital

GODOWSKY, LEOPOLD (1870-1938)

s.a. Rameau

Alt Wien [from *Triakontameron*]

4/04/30	Warsaw, Ind., Zerelda Reading Club
4/06/30	Aurora, Ill.
11/17/30	St. Joseph, Mo., Fortnightly Music Club
11/18/30	St. Louis, Progressive Series Teachers College

GOOSSENS, EUGENE (1893-1962)

March of a Wooden Soldier [from *Kaleidoscope*, Op. 18, no. 4]

    10/18/34   Rosemont, Pa., Rosemont College

GRANADOS, ENRIQUE (1867-1916)

Danse, E major

    2/22/23   Chicago, Fortnightly Music Club

Goyescas, no. 4 [1911]

11/03/26	New York, Studio Guild and WOR
7/07/27	New York, New York University
4/04/30	Warsaw, Ind., Zerelda Reading Club
4/06/30	Aurora, Ill.
4/08/30	Springfield, Ill.
4/05/42	Northampton, Mass., Smith College

Goyescas, no. 5 ["Laments, or the Lady and the Nightingale"]

8/31/27	Oldenburg, Ind., Convent of the Sisters of St. Francis
9/01/27	Oldenburg, Ind., Convent of the Sisters of St. Francis
11/17/30	St. Joseph, Mo., Fortnightly Music Club
11/18/30	St. Louis, Progressive Series Teachers College
12/11/38	Suffern, N.Y.
8/19/42	Long Island, Red Cross Benefit
3/20/47	Bronxville, N.Y., Women's Club
6/08/47	San Antonio, Our Lady of the Lake College

Playera, Spanish Dance

4/27/22	Decatur, Ill., Federation of Music Clubs
1/07/24	Medford, Ore.
1/11/24	Salem, Ore.
1/15/24	Portland, Ore.
1/17/24	Seattle, Wash.
2/27/24	Boston, MacDowell Club

3/20/24   Williamstown, Mass.

GRIFFES, CHARLES (1884-1920)

The Vale of Dreams [from *Three Tone-Pictures*, op. 5 (?1912)]

> 4/27/22   Decatur, Ill., Federation of Music Clubs
> 3/31/26   Portland, Ore.
> 4/05/26   Seattle, Wash., Women's Century Club
> 10/18/34   Rosemont, Pa., Rosemont College
> 6/08/47   San Antonio, Our Lady of the Lake College

HANSON, HOWARD (1896-1981)

Clog Dance

> 9/19/26   Woodstock, N.Y., Maverick Sunday Concerts
> 11/03/26   New York, Studio Guild and WOR
> 7/07/27   New York, New York University
> 8/31/27   Oldenburg, Ind., Convent of the Sisters of
>   St. Francis
> 9/01/27   Oldenburg, Ind., Convent of the Sisters of
>   St. Francis
> 3/05/28   New York, Columbia University
> 5/23/29   New York, Afternoon musicales
> 10/18/34   Rosemont, Pa., Rosemont College

HARRIS, ROY (1898-1979)

*Sonata for Violin and Piano [1942], with Madeleine Carabo-Cone

> 11/03/46   Northampton, Mass., Smith College
> 11/04/46   Hempstead, Long Island, Hofstra College
> 11/08/46   New York, Manhattan College; first New York
>   Performance
> 11/11/46   New York, Town Hall

*Toccata from Sonata for Violin and Piano

> 4/29/48   New York, Times Hall

HAYDN, JOSEPH (1732-1809)

Andante and Variations

2/15/25	New York, Civic Club
2/26/25	Athol, Mass.
3/05/25	Newburyport, Mass., Music Club
3/20/25	Boston
6/18/25	St. Louis, Progressive Series Teachers College
6/16/26	San Antonio, Incarnate Word College

Variations in F minor

4/27/22	Decatur, Ill., Federation of Music Clubs
5/22/39	New York, St. Walburga's Academy

HINDEMITH, PAUL (1895-1963)

Der Damon for Chamber Orchestra [1922, dance-pantomime; 1923, concert suite for small orchestra]

1/30/27	New York, Aeolian Hall, sponsored by the International Composers' Guild [Carol Robinson on celesta]

HONEGGER, ARTHUR (1892-1955)

Pièce brève no. 7 [from *Sept pièces brèves*, 1919-20]

Between 1/29 and 2/3/23	Chicago
4/23/?	New York, Anderson Galleries, with Henri

INFANTE, MANUEL (1883-1958)

Danse Gitane [from *Gitanerias*?]

10/11/33	Rosemont, Pa., Rosemont College
4/05/42	Northampton, Mass., Smith College

IVES, CHARLES (1874-1954)

*Sonata no. 3 for Piano and Violin, with Madeleine Carabo-Cone

11/03/46	Northampton, Mass., Smith College
11/04/46	Hempstead, Long Island, Hofstra College
11/08/46	New York, Manhattan College; first New York performance
11/11/46	New York, Town Hall (billed as first New York performance)
2/16/27	Brooklyn, N.Y., Brooklyn Museum Concert
4/29/48	New York, Times Hall
11/18/46	New York, broadcast on WNYC

JOHNSTONE [probably Arthur Edward Johnstone (1860-1944), composer specializing in piano methods and for a time director of the Progressive Series Teachers College, St. Louis. See *The National Cyclopedia of American Biography*, 32: 329-330.]

Kaleidoscope

6/26/25	St. Louis, Progressive Series Teachers College
6/16/26	San Antonio, Incarnate Word College

KAY, ULYSSES (1917-)

*Sonatina for Violin and Piano (1942) [According to Eileen Southern, "Kay, Ulysses," in *The New Grove Dictionary of American Music*, 2: 615-616, this Sonatina was later withdrawn]

4/29/48	New York, Times Hall, with Madeleine Carabo-Cone

[The first performance of this Sonata was apparently given by Leonard Bernstein and Stefan Franckel at the League of Composers' concert of works by composers in the Armed Forces, 1/24/43.]

LISZT, FRANZ (1811-1886)
s.a. Schumann-Liszt, Bach-Liszt

Gnomenreigen [also cited as "Dance of the Gnomes," no. 2 of Two Concert Etudes]

2/26/20	Highland Park, Ill.
2/22/23	Chicago, Fortnightly Music Club
12/18/23	Boston, Boston University
8/30/25	Glencoe, Ill.
10/14/25	Mt. Carroll, Ill.
10/19/25	Springfield, Ill.
10/21/25	Decatur, Ill.
1/28/26	Millbrook, N.Y., Bennett School
3/15/26	Aurora, Ill.
3/17/26	Lawrence, Kan., University of Kansas
3/21/26	San Antonio, Our Lady of the Lake College
4/25/26	Pullman, Wash., State College of Washington
7/07/27	New York, New York University
5/15/27	?, Douglaston Club
8/31/27	Oldenburg, Ind., Convent of the Sisters of St. Francis
9/01/27	Oldenburg, Ind., Convent of the Sisters of St. Francis
3/04/28	New York, Columbia University
10/18/34	Rosemont, Pa., Rosemont College
1/24/36	Millbrook, N.Y., Bennett School
12/11/38	Suffern, N.Y.
4/04/39	Peoria, Ill.
7/25/40	Centerville, Mass.
3/20/47	Bronxville, N.Y., Women's Club
6/08/47	San Antonio, Our Lady of the Lake College

Etude, D-flat major [from Three Concert Etudes]

11/01/16	Chicago
Between 1/29 and 2/3/23	Chicago
3/29/26	Salem, Ore., Civic Music Club
3/31/26	Portland, Ore.
4/05/26	Seattle, Wash., Women's Century Club
4/13/26	Medford, Ore., Andrews Conservatory

Etude, F minor [from Three Concert Etudes]

1/03/22	Rogers Park, Ill., Women's Club
4/27/22	Decatur, Ill., Federation of Music Clubs
12/18/23	Boston, Boston University
1/07/24	Medford, Ore.
1/11/24	Salem, Ore.
1/15/24	Portland, Ore.
1/17/24	Seattle, Wash.
3/04/24	Boston, Steinert Hall
8/30/25	Glencoe, Ill.
10/14/25	Mt. Carroll, Ill.
10/19/25	Springfield, Ill.
10/21/25	Decatur, Ill.
1/28/26	Millbrook, N.Y., Bennett School
3/15/26	Aurora, Ill.
3/17/26	Lawrence, Kan., University of Kansas
3/21/26	San Antonio, Our Lady of the Lake College
4/25/26	Pullman, Wash., State College of Washington
7/07/27	New York, New York University
8/31/27	Oldenburg, Ind., Convent of the Sisters of St. Francis
9/01/27	Oldenburg, Ind., Convent of the Sisters of St. Francis
3/10/29	Paris, American Women's Club
11/01/29	Albany, N.Y., Women's Club
12/10/29	Emmitsburg, Md.
3/22/39	Rosemont, Pa., Rosemont College
4/04/39	Peoria, Ill.
3/20/47	Bronxville, N.Y.
6/08/47	San Antonio, Our Lady of the Lake College
12/11/55	New York, Museum of the City of N.Y.

Gondoliera [from *Années de pèlerinage*]

4/04/30	Warsaw, Ind., Zerelda Reading Club
4/06/30	Aurora, Ill.
4/08/30	Springfield, Ill.
11/17/30	St. Joseph, Mo., Fortnightly Music Club
11/18/30	St. Louis, Progressive Series Teachers College

*Hungarian Phantasy [*sic*] for Piano and Orchestra [*Fantasie über ungarische Volksmelodien*]

    10/09/25   Worcester, Mass., Worcester Music Festival [first Festival performance]

Rhapsody no. 14 [F minor]

10/26/24	Chicago, Playhouse
1/20/25	Springfield, Ill.
2/26/25	Athol, Mass.
3/05/25	Newburyport, Mass., Music Club
3/20/25	Boston, Mass.
10/11/33	Rosemont, Pa., Rosemont College

Witches' Dance [presumably, the transcription of the fifth movement of Berlioz' *Symphonie fantastique, Songe d'une nuit du Sabbath*]

1/07/24	Medford, Ore.
1/11/24	Salem, Ore.
1/15/24	Portland, Ore.
1/17/24	Seattle, Wash.
3/04/24	Boston, Steinert Hall
3/20/24	Williamstown, Mass.

MACDOWELL, EDWARD (1860-1908)

Brer Rabbit [*Of Br'er Rabbit*, from *Fireside Tales*, 1901-02]

11/20/16	New York, Comedy Theatre
10/11/33	Rosemont, Pa., Rosemont College

Concert Etude [*Étude de concert*, 1887]

2/26/21	Chicago, Leon Mandel Hall
5/15/27	?, Douglaston Club
7/07/27	New York, New York University
8/31/27	Oldenburg, Ind., Convent of the Sisters of St. Francis
9/01/27	Oldenburg, Ind., Convent of the Sisters of St. Francis

*Concerto for Pianoforte, Op. 15, [A minor, 1882; premiered by MacDowell in 1894]

2/18 and	Chicago, with the Chicago Symphony Orchestra,
2/19/21	Frederick Stock conducting

Moonshine [*Mondschein*, from *Vier kleine Poesien*, 1887]

2/26/25	Athol, Mass.
3/05/25	Newburyport, Mass., Music Club
3/20/25	Boston
3/21/26	San Antonio, Our Lady of the Lake College
3/29/26	Salem, Ore., Civic Music Club
4/13/26	Medford, Ore., Andrews Conservatory

Winter [after Shelley, from *Vier kleine Poesien*, 1887]

2/26/25	Athol, Mass.
3/05/25	Newburyport, Mass., Music Club
3/20/25	Boston
3/21/26	San Antonio, Our Lady of the Lake College
3/29/26	Salem, Ore., Civic Music Club
4/13/26	Medford, Ore., Andrews Conservatory
10/11/33	Rosemont, Pa., Rosemont College

MARTINŮ, BOHUSLAV (1890-1959)

Par T.S.F.

4/18/26	Portland, Ore., Pro-Musica Concert
9/19/26	Woodstock, N.Y., Maverick Sunday Concerts
12/30/28	Paris, Students and Artists' Club
5/23/29	New York, Afternoon musicales

MENDELSSOHN, FELIX (1809-1847)

Hunting Song

1/24/36	Millbrook, N.Y., Bennett School

Scherzo, E minor [from *Trois Fantasies*, Op. 16, no. 1]

    3/22/39   Rosemont, Pa., Rosemont College

MILHAUD, DARIUS (1892-1974)

Sumaré [*Saudades do Brazil*, vol. II, no. 4]

    2/22/23   Chicago, Fortnightly Music Club
    1/07/24   Medford, Ore.
    1/11/24   Salem, Ore.
    1/15/24   Portland, Ore.
    1/17/24   Seattle, Wash.
    3/04/24   Boston; first Boston performance
    6/26/25   St. Louis, Progressive Series Teachers College
    4/25/26   Pullman, Wash., State College of Washington

MOZART, WOLFGANG AMADEUS (1756-1791)

Larghetto, A major

    7/25/40   Centerville, Mass.

*Quintet, for Piano, Oboe, Clarinet, Horn and Bassoon, K. 452 [E-flat]

    4/25/56   New York, Dalcroze Faculty Recital

*Sonata in D [for two pianos, available Schirmer, ed. E. Hughes]

    8/08/40   Centerville, Mass.

MUSSORGSKY, MODEST (1839-1881)

Boris Godounow [sic] "transcription by Carol Robinson"

    2/26/25   Athol, Mass.
    3/05/25   Newburyport, Mass., Music Club
    3/20/25   Boston, Mass.

*Coronation Scene from *Boris* [arr. Lee Pattison for two pianos, available Schirmer]

    8/08/40   Centerville, Mass.

PADEREWSKI, IGNACY JAN (1860-1941)

Cracovienne fantastique [Op. 14, 1888]

    2/26/20   Highland Park, Ill.

PALMGREN, SELIM (1878-1951)

The Swan [from *6 Lyric Pieces*, Op. 28]

    2/26/21   Chicago, Leon Mandel Hall

PIZZETTI, ILDEBRANDO (1880-1968)

*Trio in A [1925]

    11/28/26   New York, Aeolian Hall, International Composers' Guild

POULENC, FRANCIS (1899-1963)

Mouvements perpétuels [1918]

    4/23/?   New York Anderson Galleries, with Henri

Promenades [1921]

    3/04/24   Boston, Steinert Hall, First Boston performance
    10/26/24   Chicago, Playhouse
    1/20/25   Springfield, Ill.
    2/15/25   New York, Civic Club
    2/26/25   Athol, Mass.
    3/05/25   Newburyport, Mass., Music Club

6/26/25	St. Louis, Progressive Series Teachers College; only two movements: À pied, En cheval
3/31/26	Portland, Ore.
4/05/26	Seattle, Wash., Women's Century Club: À pied, En cheval, En diligence
5/23/29	New York, Afternoon musicales

Valse

2/22/23	Chicago, Fortnightly Music Club

PROKOFIEV, SERGEI (1891-1953)

Vision[s] *fugitive*[s] [Op. 22, 1915-17]

3/04/28	New York, Columbia University
5/23/29	New York, Afternoon musicales

RAKHMANINOV, SERGEI (1873-1943)

Prelude, G-sharp minor [Op. 32, no. 12]

3/22/39	Rosemont, Pa., Rosemont College
4/04/39	Peoria, Ill.

Romance (Lilacs)

2/22/23	Chicago, Fortnightly Music Club

RAMEAU-GODOWSKY

Sarabande

4/27/22	Decatur, Ill., Federation of Music Clubs Fifth Annual Meeting
10/21/36	Rosemont, Pa., Rosemont College

RAVEL, MAURICE (1875-1937)

Alborada (del gracioso) [from *Miroirs*, 1904-05]

     10/11/33   Rosemont, Pa., Rosemont College
     2/14/38   New York, St. Walburga's Academy

*Ma mere l'oye (for two pianos) [1908-1910]

     8/08/40   Centerville, Mass.

Ondine [from *Gaspard de la nuit*, 1908]

     2/26/20   Highland Park, Ill.
     12/18/23   Boston, Boston University
     1/07/24   Medford, Ore.
     1/11/24   Salem, Ore.
     1/15/24   Portland, Ore.
     1/17/24   Seattle, Wash.
     3/04/24   Boston, Mass.
     6/26/25   St. Louis, Progressive Series Teachers College
     7/12/25   San Antonio, Our Lady of the Lake College
     10/14/25   Mt. Carroll, Ill.
     10/19/25   Springfield, Ill.
     10/21/25   Decatur, Ill.
     12/30/28   Paris, Students and Artists' Club
     5/23/29   New York, Afternoon musicales
     10/18/34   Rosemont, Pa., Rosemont College
     7/25/40   Centerville, Mass.
     4/23/?   New York, Anderson Galleries, with Henri

ROBINSON, CAROL (1890-1979)

Capriccio

     n.d., recorded on Welte C-7471, "The Masters on Your Piano."

Prelude and Capriccio, 1917

     2/15/25   New York, Civic Club
     2/26/25   Athol, Mass.
     3/05/25   Newburyport, Mass., Music Club

  3/20/25   Boston, Mass.

Prelude, C major

  12/11/38   Suffern, New York

Prelude, E-flat minor [Dedicated to Fannie Bloomfield-Zeisler, (1919)]

  7/12/34   Rosemont, Pa., Rosemont College
  12/11/38   Suffern, N.Y.

Prelude, F-sharp minor (1919)

  12/11/38   Suffern, New York
  n.d., recorded on Welte C-7471, "The Masters on Your Piano."

SAINT-SAËNS, CAMILLE (1835-1921)

Toccata

  4/04/30   Warsaw, Ind., Zerelda Reading Club
  4/06/30   Aurora, Ill.
  4/08/30   Springfield, Ill.
  11/17/30   St. Joseph, Mo., Fortnightly Music Club
  11/18/30   St. Louis, Progressive Series Teachers College

SATIE, ERIK (1866-1925)

Air du Grand Prieur [*Sonneries de la Rose + Croix*, no. 3]

  7/25/40   Centerville, Mass.

Third Gymnopédie [1888]

  9/19/26   Woodstock, N.Y., Maverick Sunday Concerts

SCARLATTI, DOMENICO (1685-1757)

Pastorale

6/18/25	St. Louis, Progressive Series Teachers College
8/30/25	Glencoe, Ill.
10/14/25	Mt. Carroll, Ill.
10/19/25	Springfield, Ill.
10/21/25	Decatur, Ill.
1/28/26	Millbrook, N.Y., Bennett School
3/15/26	Aurora, Ill.
3/21/26	San Antonio, Our Lady of the Lake College
3/29/26	Salem, Ore., Civic Music Club
3/31/26	Portland, Ore.
4/05/26	Seattle, Wash., Women's Century Club
4/13/26	Medford, Ore., Andrews Conservatory
4/25/26	Pullman, Wash., State College of Washington
6/16/26	San Antonio, Incarnate Word College
7/10 or	Oldenburg, Ind., Convent of the Sisters of
7/11/26	St. Francis
7/12/26	San Antonio, Our Lady of the Lake College
3/17/27	Lawrence, Kan., University of Kansas
3/04/28	New York, Columbia University
1/17/?	New York, Fifth Avenue Playhouse

Sonata, A minor

9/19/26	Woodstock, N.Y., Maverick Sunday Concerts

Sonata, C minor

9/19/26	Woodstock, N.Y., Maverick Sunday Concerts
2/14/28	New York, St. Walburga's Academy
10/18/34	Rosemont, Pa., Rosemont College
12/11/38	Suffern, N.Y.

Sonata, E major

2/14/28	New York, St. Walburga's Academy
12/11/38	Suffern, N.Y.
4/04/39	Peoria, Ill.
3/20/40	Bronxville, N.Y., Women's Club
7/25/40	Centerville, Mass.

Sonata, E minor

    2/14/28   New York, St. Walburga's Academy

Sonata, F major

    2/14/28   New York, St. Walburga's Academy
   10/18/34   Rosemont, Pa., Rosemont College
    7/25/40   Centerville, Mass.

SCHUBERT, FRANZ (1797-1828)

Fantasie, Op. 103, F minor [1828, for four hands]

    4/05/57   Dalcroze Faculty Recital

Impromptu, Op. 90, no. 4 [A-flat major]

    4/04/30   Warsaw, Ind., Zerelda Reading Club
    4/06/30   Aurora, Ill.

Minuet, Op. 78 [from Sonata in G major, 1827]

    6/18/25   St. Louis, Progressive Series Teachers College

SCHUBERT-GANZ [Rudolf Ganz (1877-1972), Swiss-born pianist, conductor, and teacher, was a pupil of Busoni and led a significant and varied career in the United States from 1901 until his death.]

Ballet music from *Rosamunde*

    1/03/22   Rogers Park, Ill., Women's Club
    4/27/22   Decatur, Ill., Federation of Music Clubs
    7/07/27   New York, New York University
    8/31/27   Oldenburg, Ind., Convent of the Sisters of
                    St. Francis
    9/01/27   Oldenburg, Ind., Convent of the Sisters of
                    St. Francis
    3/04/28   New York, Columbia University
    3/22/39   Rosemont, Pa., Rosemont College
    5/22/39   New York, St. Walburga's Academy

SCHUBERT-LISZT

Soirrée [sic] *de Vienne*

    10/21/36   Rosemont, Pa., Rosemont College

SCHUMANN, ROBERT (1810-1856)

Andante and Variations, Op. 46 [B-flat major; 1843; for two pianos, ed. for Schirmer by E. Hughes]

    8/08/40   Centerville, Mass.
    4/05/57   New York, Dalcroze Faculty Recital

Arabesque [Op. 18, c. 1838]

    4/04/30   Warsaw, Ind., Zerelda Reading Club
    4/06/30   Aurora, Ill.
  11/17/30   St. Joseph, Mo., Fortnightly Music Club
  11/18/30   St. Louis, Progressive Series Teachers College
    1/24/36   Millbrook, N.Y., Bennett School

Phantasiestücke, Op. 73 for Clarinet and Piano [1849; violin/cello *ad libitum*]

    4/05/57   Dalcroze Faculty Recital

Prophet Bird [*Vogel als Prophet* from *Waldscenen*, Op. 82]

  12/11/38   Suffern, N.Y.
    8/19/42   Long Island, Red Cross Benefit

*Quartet in E-flat, Op. 47, for piano, violin, viola, cello

    1/25/53   New York, Dalcroze Faculty Recital

Sonata [no. 2], Op. 22, G minor

  11/01/16   Chicago

11/20/16	New York, Comedy Theatre
2/16/20	Highland Park, Ill.
1/07/24	Medford, Ore.
1/11/24	Salem, Ore.
1/15/24	Portland, Oregon
1/17/24	Seattle, Wash.
3/04/24	Boston, Steinert Hall
3/20/24	Williamstown, Mass.
7/07/27	New York, New York University
8/31/27	Oldenburg, Ind., Convent of the Sisters of St. Francis
9/01/27	Oldenburg, Ind., Convent of the Sisters of St. Francis
11/01/29	Albany, N.Y., Women's Club, *Allegro* only
4/08/30	Springfield, Ill.
4/05/42	Northampton, Mass., Smith College
8/19/42	Long Island, Red Cross Benefit
3/20/47	Bronxville, N.Y., Women's Club
6/08/47	San Antonio, Our Lady of the Lake College
12/11/55	New York, Museum of the City of N.Y., *Allegro* only

Warum [from *Phantasiestücke*, Op. 12]

| 4/04/30 | Warsaw, Ind., Zerelda Reading Club |

SCHUMANN-LISZT

Bird as Prophet [*Vogel als Prophet* from *Waldscenen*, Op. 82]

| 10/21/36 | Rosemont, Pa., Rosemont College |
| 4/04/39 | Peoria, Ill. |

Dedication [*Widmung*, 1848]

3/20/24	Williamstown, Mass.
3/21/24	Worcester, Mass., Mechanics Hall
12/30/28	Paris, Students and Artists' Club
2/14/38	New York, St. Walburga's Academy

Frülingsnacht [*Überm Garten durch die Lüfte*, 1872]

| 3/21/24 | Worcester, Mass., Mechanics Hall |

5/15/27	?, Douglaston Club
12/09/28	Paris, Students' Atelier
7/12/34	Rosemont, Pa., Rosemont College
2/14/38	New York, St. Walburga's Academy
8/19/42	Long Island, Red Cross Benefit

*SCHÜTT, EDWARD (1856-1933)

Suite no. 1, D minor

> 3/17/15   Chicago, Fine Arts Building, with Josephine Gerwig, violin

SEARS, HELEN [d. 1933]

Sketch

> 2/26/20   Highland Park, Ill.

SINDING, CHRISTIAN (1856-1941)

Caprice [from 15 *Caprices*, Op. 44, 1898?]

> 6/27/26   San Antonio, Our Lady of the Lake College
> 7/10 or   Oldenburg, Ind., Convent of the Sisters of
> 7/11/26   St. Francis

SKRYABIN, ALEXANDER (1872-1915)

Poème, Op. 31, no. 2 [Op. 32 is *Deux poèmes*, dated 1903. Op. 31 is the Four preludes. Under the Op. 31 number, the following performances took place:]

> 3/20/24   Williamstown, Mass.
> 3/21/24   Worcester, Mass., Mechanics Hall
> 3/15/26   Aurora, Ill.
> 4/25/26   Pullman, Wash., State College of Washington
> 7/07/27   New York, New York University
> 8/31/27   Oldenburg, Ind., Convent of the Sisters of
>   St. Francis

9/01/27	Oldenburg, Ind., Convent of the Sisters of St. Francis
5/23/29	New York, Afternoon musicales
1/17/?	New York, Fifth Avenue Playhouse

Poème, Op. 32, no. 2

4/27/22	Decatur, Ill., Federation of Music Clubs
12/18/23	Boston, Boston University
1/07/24	Medford, Ore.
1/11/24	Salem, Ore.
1/15/24	Portland, Ore.
1/17/24	Seattle, Wash.
3/04/24	Boston
6/26/25	St. Louis, Progressive Series Teachers College
7/12/25	San Antonio, Our Lady of the Lake College
10/14/25	Mt. Carroll, Ill.
10/19/25	Springfield, Ill.
10/21/25	Decatur, Ill.
1/28/26	Millbrook, N.Y., Bennett School
3/17/26	Lawrence, Kan., University of Kansas
3/04/28	New York, Columbia University
4/23/?	New York, Anderson Galleries, with Henri

Poème in D major

| 1/03/22 | Rogers Park, Ill., Women's Club |

STEINERT, ALEXANDER [LANG] JR. (1900-1982)

Danse exotique (1922)

Between 1/29 and 2/3/23	Chicago
12/18/23	Boston, Mass.
1/07/24	Medford, Ore.
1/11/24	Salem, Ore. [An Oregon review of this performance, GU MS 300, calls the occasion a "premier."]
1/15/24	Portland, Ore.
1/17/24	Seattle, Wash.
3/04/24	Boston, Steinert Hall

3/20/24	Williamstown, Mass.
3/21/24	Worcester, Mass., Mechanics Hall
10/26/24	Chicago, Playhouse
1/20/25	Springfield, Ill.
2/15/25	New York, Civic Club
2/26/25	Athol, Mass.
3/05/25	Newburyport, Mass., Music Club
4/23/?	New York, Anderson Galleries with Henri

STRAUSS, RICHARD (1864-1949)

Reverie [presumably *Träumerei* from Op. 9, *Stimmungsbilder*]

      6/16/26   San Antonio, Incarnate Word College

*Sonata [Op. 18] E-flat major

      3/17/15   Chicago, Fine Arts Building, with Josephine Gerwig, violin

STRAVINSKY, IGOR (1882-1971)

Chez Petrouchka [Three movements from *Petrushka*, 1921]

12/18/23	Boston, Boston University
1/07/24	Medford, Ore.
1/11/24	Salem, Ore.
1/15/24	Portland, Ore.
1/17/24	Seattle, Wash.
3/04/24	Boston, Steinert Hall
10/26/24	Chicago, Playhouse
1/20/25	Springfield, Ill.
2/15/25	New York, Civic Club
2/26/25	Athol, Mass.
3/05/25	Newburyport, Mass., Music Club
6/26/25	St. Louis, Progressive Series Teachers College
9/19/26	Woodstock, N.Y., Maverick Sunday Concerts
12/09/28	Paris, Students' Atelier
5/23/29	New York, Afternoon musicales
11/01/29	Albany, N.Y., Women's Club
11/17/30	St. Joseph, Mo., Fortnightly Music Club

    7/25/40   Centerville, Mass.
    4/05/42   Northampton, Mass., Smith College

Petrouchka, transcribed by the composer for four hands

    4/18/26   Portland, Ore., Pro-Musica Concert

TCHAIKOVSKY, PETER ILYICH (1840-1893)

*Piano Concerto no. 1 in B-flat minor, Op. 23 [1875]

    2/26/24   Providence, R.I., with the Boston Symphony
                   Orchestra
    10/21/25   New Haven, Conn., with the Philharmonic Society
                   of New York, van Hoogstraten conducting, under
                   the auspices of the Yale School of Music
    10/23/25   Worcester, Mass., as above

VERACINI, FRANCESCO MARIA (1690-c. 1768)

*Sonata in E major for piano and violin

    6/27/26   San Antonio, Our Lady of the Lake College

VINCI, LEONARDO (1690-1730)

Largo

    3/22/39   Rosemont, Pa., Rosemont College
    4/04/39   Peoria, Ill.
    5/22/39   New York, St. Walburga's Academy

WHITFIELD, KATHRYN [Thomas]

In an Irish Jaunting Car [published by Schirmer c. 1920 for violin and
piano as well as for piano solo]

    2/26/21   Chicago, Leon Mandel Hall
    1/07/24   Medford, Ore.

1/11/24	Salem, Ore.
1/15/24	Portland, Ore.
1/17/24	Seattle, Wash.
2/27/24	Boston, MacDowell Club

APPENDIX B

COMPOSITIONS BY CAROL ROBINSON

In this appendix appear compositions by Carol Robinson preceded by a Works List. An asterisk indicates that the work is known only by citation on a program or in correspondence. Copies of the remaining works may be found in GU. Few are dated. Where either composition dates or performances are known, these are given.

WORKS LIST

Art Songs

The name of the poet follows the song in parenthesis.

April song (Sara Teasdale)

2/26/20	Highland Park, Ill., Anna Burmeister, soprano
5/22/?	Chicago, Kimball Hall, Anna Burmeister, soprano
10/20/?	New York, Aeolian Hall

The Daisies (James Stephens). To Gloria Caruso and Michael Hunt Murray

5/06/47	Butler, Pa., The Tuesday Musical Club, performed during National Music Week, Arthur van Haelst, soloist
5/09/57	+Canton, Pa., Arthur van Haelst, soloist

The Lamb (William Blake)

Loveliest of Trees (Alfred E. Housman). To Arthur van Haelst

    5/06/47   Butler, Pa., The Tuesday Musical Club; National
                     Music Week; Arthur van Haelst, soloist
    5/09/47   +Canton, Pa., Arthur van Haelst, soloist

Mary's Pity (Praised in a letter of 13 December 1919 to Robinson from James Rogers, Cleveland, Oh., GU MS 300, Box 1, Folder 2)

Never More Will the Wind (H.D.)

Shadowy Woodlands (Fiona Macleod). To Anna Burmeister

    2/26/20   Highland Park, Ill., Anna Burmeister, soprano
    4/25/22   Decatur, Ill., under the auspices of the Illinois
                     Federation of Music Clubs, Anna Burmeister,
                     soprano
    5/11/?   Chicago, Kimball Hall, Anna Burmeister, soprano
    10/20/?   New York, Aeolian Hall

Silence of Amor (Fiona Macleod), composed 1914. NFMC Prizewinner [1918?] for best art song by an American composer

    2/26/20   Highland Park, Ill., Anna Burmeister, soprano

Two Poems by Emily Dickinson:

  I'll Tell You How the Sun Rose

  The Moon Was But a Chin of Gold

Velvet Shoes (Elinor Wylie)

+Sponsors of the concert in Canton included the Beethoven Club of Canton, the Mendelssohn Club of Canton, the Evening Musicale of Canton and the Etude Club of Leroy.

Choral Works

Carol, Children's Christmas Song (Kenneth Grahame, from *The Wind in the Willows*)

To Spring (William Blake), to the Taliesin Singers, TTBB

Works for Piano Solo

Inventions, etudes, duets and other pieces composed for her students are omitted as are transcriptions.

*Capriccio, recorded by Robinson on "The Master's Fingers on Your Piano," C-7471

Chorale Dance, for Elizabeth Delza, composed December, 1945

*First Partita in B-flat

Legend, for Harriet Todd, composed December, 1945

> 3/12/46   Peoria, Ill., The Amateur Musical Club,
> Harriet Todd, soloist

Pastorale

*Prelude in C major

> 12/11/38   Suffern, N.Y., by Carol Robinson

Prelude in E-flat minor, to Fannie Bloomfield Zeisler, composed 1919

      7/12/34   Rosemont, Pa., Carol Robinson, soloist

Prelude in F-sharp minor, composed 1919, recorded by Robinson on "The Master's Fingers on Your Piano," C-7471

*Two Intermezzi

THE MUSIC

The works that follow are arranged alphabetically within the larger categories of art song, choral music, and keyboard music. They are produced here with the permission of the Robinson Estate. All of Robinson's known works are included in this edition with the exception of inventions, etudes, and exercises composed for her students and transcriptions. An example of her etudes for students may be seen on pages 37-38, where *Pedagogical Exercise No. 4* is reproduced.

The Daisies

(𝅘𝅥𝅭 = 54) Allegretto

In the scent-ed bud of the morn-ing-O, when the
win - dy grass went rip-pling far, I saw my dear one
walk - ing slow, In the field where the dai - sies are.___

We did not laugh_____ and

The Lamb

tell thee; Lit-tle lamb I'll tell thee. He is call-d by thy

name, For He calls him-self a Lamb;

He is meek and He is mild,

He be-came a lit-tle child___ I a child and thou a lamb

Loveliest of Trees

bout the wood-lands I will go to see the cher-ry hung with snow

Never More Will the Wind

gone, and you are flown: Like a bird out of our hand, like a light out of our heart, You are gone.

Shadowy Woodlands

A - cross the sha - dow - y wood - lands I⏤ hear the voice of the cuck - oo⏤ Sail-ing like⏤ a sil - ver skiff⏤ up-on the moon - flood.⏤

of the wood,

the moon - light sleeps.

Silence of Amor

In the hol-lows of qui-et pla-ces we may meet, the qui-et

pla - ces__ where__ is nei - ther moon__ nor sun,__ but

on - ly the light as of am - ber and pale gold__

that comes from the Hills of the Heart.__

grass,___ at the ris-ing of the moon.___

I'll Tell You How The Sun Rose

I'll tell you how the sun rose, a rib-bon at a time, The
stee-ples swam in am-e-thyst, The news like squir-rels ran.
The hills un-tied their bon-nets The bob-o-links be-gun, Then
I said soft-ly to my-self, "That must have been the sun."

But how he set I know not, there seemed a pur-ple stile which lit-tle yel-low boys & girls were clim-bing all the while till when they reached the oth-er side A

dom - i - nie in gray put gen-tly up the eve-ning bars___

rit. & dim. - ᒣ

___ and led the flock a - way.

The Moon Was But a Chin of Gold

The moon was but a chin of gold a night or two a-go, And

now she turns her per-fect face up-on the world be - low. Her

fore - head is of am - plest blond; Her

cheek like ber - yl stone;_____ Her

what a pri-vi-lege to— be but the re-mot-est star! For

cer-tain-ly her way might pass Be-side your twink-ling door. Her

bon - net is the firm-a-ment, The un - i - verse her shoe, The

rall.

stars the trin-kets at her belt, Her dim - i-ties of blue.____

Velvet Shoes

Carol

Here we stand in the cold & the sleet, Blow-ing fin-gers to stamp - ing feet, Come from far a - way you to greet___ You by the fire___ and we in the street Bid-ding you joy in the morn - ing! For

ere one half of the night was gone, sud-den a star has led us on, Rain-ing bliss____ and ben-i-son____ Bliss to-mor-row and more a-non Joy for ev-er-y morn-ing! Good man Jo-seph

toiled through the snow, saw the star o'er a sta-ble low;

Ma-ry she might not furth-er go Wel-come thatch, and

lit-ter be-low! Joy was hers in the morn_ing!

And then they heard the

To Spring

*piano reduction for rehearsal only

val-leys hear; All our long-ing eyes are turned up to thy bright pa-vi-lions;

val-leys hear; All our long-ing eyes are turned up to thy bright pa-vi-lions;

All our long-ing eyes are turned up to thy bright pa-vi-lions;

Is - sue forth and let thy

Is - sue forth and let thy

Is - sue forth and let thy

Is - sue forth and let thy

200

Chorale Dance for Elizabeth Delza

Legend

Pastorale

Prelude in E♭ minor

Prelude in F#minor

APPENDIX C

WELTE PIANO ROLLS MADE BY CAROL ROBINSON

Location of playable copies is currently unknown.

July, 1925

B 1578	MacDowell, *Woodland Sketches*
B 2662	MacDowell, *By a Meadow Brook*
C 7105	MacDowell, *Winter and Moonshine*, from *Four Little Poems*, Op. 34, nos. 3 and 4

September, 1925

C 7147	De Falla, *Andaluza*

February, 1926

C 7275	Liszt, *Hungarian Rhapsody*, no. 14
X 7145	Alaleona, arranger: *Italian Song of the 16th Century*
X 7148	Schütt, Prelude to *Carnaval Mignon Suite*, Op. 48, no. 1
X 7146	Debussy, Second *Arabesque*
C 7062	Beecher, Waltz in B-flat minor

March, 1926

C 7293	Mussorgsky-Frühling, Fantasy on Themes from *Boris Godunov*

October, 1926

Granados, *Playera* (Spanish Dance no. 5)

November, 1926

C 7471   Robinson, Gigue from *First Partita* in B-flat

Date uncertain

C 7471   Robinson, Capriccio
                Robinson, Prelude in F-sharp minor

SELECTED BIBLIOGRAPHY

Manuscripts

Private Papers

Elizabeth Delza Papers. Correspondence, programs, and music manuscripts.

David and Eleanor Robinson Papers. Assorted programs, photographs, correspondence, including letters from Frank Lloyd Wright and A. R. Orage, and family memorabilia from the nephew of Carol Robinson.

Phoebe Sells Papers. Newspaper clippings, photographs, press comments, and family history from the niece of Carol Robinson.

Library Collections

Manuscript sigla are borrowed from Donald Krummel et al., *Resources of American Music History* (Urbana: University of Illinois Press, 1981).

Cty-Yale University, New Haven, Connecticut, John Herrick Jackson Music Library, Charles E. Ives personal papers.

DLC-C-Library of Congress, Washington, D.C., George Antheil, Manuscript materials.

DLC-H-Library of Congress, Washington, D.C., Modern Music Archives.

GU-University of Georgia, Athens, Georgia, Hargrett Rare Book and Manuscript Library.

MS 300-The Carol Robinson Collection. Acquired 1969-70. Four boxes and a separate music folder containing programs, newspaper clippings, teaching notes, correspondence, and music manuscripts (these are listed separately under "Music: Manuscripts").

MS 688-The Olin Downes Papers. Acquired 1965. The Downes
Papers include correspondence, lectures, and newspaper clippings.
Approximately two-thirds of the collection has been classified into
Correspondence and Subject files, for which Jean Réti-Forbes
made an annotated inventory. The Papers are described in her
article "The Olin Downes Papers," *Georgia Review* 21 (1967):
165-171.

MS 912-The Jean Réti-Forbes Papers. Acquired 1977. These
papers include correspondence with composers and conductors,
lecture notes, tapes, photographs, and personal materials, including
information pertaining to Rudolf Réti. A typed inventory exists in
the Hargrett Library.

General Sources

Articles

Anderton, [*sic*] Margaret. "What Women are Doing for Music in America." *The Musician* 34 (1929): 33-34.

Babbitt, Milton. "Musical America's Several Generations." *Saturday
Review of Literature* 37 (1954): 36.

Babitz, Sol. "American Violin Music in the Twentieth Century."
International Musician (June 1949): 20-22.

Bauer, Emilie Frances. "Woman's Work in Music." *Etude* 20 (1902):
464.

Bauer, Marion, and Claire R. Reis. "Twenty-five Years with the League
of Composers." *Musical Quarterly* 34 (1948): 1-14.

Bernard, Elisabeth. "Jules Pasdeloup et les Concerts populaires." *Revue
de musicologie* 57 (1971): 150-178.

Brown, C. B. "Amateur Musical Clubs." *Etude* 12 (1984): 249.

C. H. "Carabo and Robinson Offer Joint Program." *The New York
Times*, 30 April 1948, p. 27.

Clark, Frances Eliot. "The Story of American Musical Clubs." *Etude* 40 (1922): 161-162.

Coeuroy, André. "Les premiers essais de musique radiogénique." *La Revue musicale* 11 (1930): 11-22.

Cortot, Alfred. "L'oeuvre pianistique d'Albert Roussel." *La Revue musicale.* Numéro spécial de *La Revue musicale* à la mémoire d'Albert Roussel 18 (1937): 293-308.

"Delza-Munson, Elizabeth." *Who's Who in America.* 44th ed. Wilmette, Illinois: Marquis Who's Who, 1986, I: 686.

[Downes, Olin]. "Music: The League of Composers." *The New York Times*, 17 November 1924, p. 17.

Downes, Olin. "Music: Pro-Musica Society." *The New York Times*, 30 January 1927, p. 28.

Dumesnil, René. "La Musique et le Machinisme." *Mercure de France* 207 (1928): 611-627.

Fay, Amy. "The Amateur Musical Clubs." *Etude* 5 (1887): 180.

"Five Concerts a Day." *The New York Times*, 4 April 1921, p. 13.

Hallock, Mary. "Women's Music Clubs." *The Musician* 16 (1911): 581, 632.

"Hartmann, Thomas de." *Baker's Biographical Dictionary of Musicians.* Ed. by Theodore Baker. Revised by Nicolas Slonimsky. 7th ed. New York: Schirmer, 1984, p. 959.

Hartmann, Thomas v. "Über die Anarchie in der Musik." *Der Blaue Reiter* (1912): 88-94.

Held, Ernst. "Women's Amateur Musical Clubs." *Etude* 12 (1894): 80.

Kimball, Alice Mary with assistance from Carol Robinson. "Fannie Bloomfield Zeisler 1863-1927." *The News Bulletin of the Leschetizky Association of America* 16 (1958): 6, 13.

Kroeger, Ernest R. "The Progress of the Middle West in Musical Art." *Etude* 17 (1899): 145.

Lott, R. Allen. "'New Music for New Ears': The International Com-posers' Guild." *Journal of the American Musicological Society* 36 (1983): 266-286.

Mâche, François-Bernard. "Schaeffer, Pierre." *The New Grove Dic-tionary of Music and Musicians.* London: Macmillan, 1980, 16: 586.

New York Herald Tribune, 21 November 1940; 12 November 1946; 30 April 1948.

The New York Times, 21 November 1916; 4 April 1921; 29 January 1928; 26 April 1933; 23 October 1938; 18 June 1939; 15 August, 14 November, 31 December 1943; 28 October 1945; 12 November 1946; 30 April 1948; 7 January, 27 May, 3 June 1951; 8 January 1952; 13 January, 16 January, 30 November 1955.

Perlis, Vivian. "Pro-musica." *The New Grove Dictionary of Music and Musicians.* Ed. Stanley Sadie. London: Macmillan, 1980, 15: 303-304.

_____. "Pro-Musica Society." *The New Grove Dictionary of American Music.* Ed. H. Wiley Hitchcock and Stanley Sadie. London: Macmillan, 1986, 3: 633-634.

Raven-Hart, R. "La Musique et la T.S.F." *La Revue musicale* 11 (1930): 1-10.

Royer, Étienne. "La Musique et la T.S.F." *La Revue musicale* 5 (1924): 157-158.

"Ruth Bradley Opens New York Studio." *Musical America*, 10 November 1936, p. 33.

Seiberling, Mrs. Frank A. "What the National Federation of Musical Clubs is Doing to Help in Making America a Musical Nation." *Etude* 40 (1922): 157-158.

Shackleford, Rudy. "The Yaddo Festivals of American Music, 1932-1952." *Perspectives of New Music* 17 (1987): 92-125.

Smith, Fanny Morris. "Woman's Work in Music." *Etude* 19 (1901): 150-151.

Troendle, Theodora. "How Fannie Bloomfield Zeisler Taught." *Etude* 47 (1929): 799-800.

Turner, Chittenden. "Music and the Women's Crusade." *Arts and Decoration* 19 (1923): 29, 70-73.

Twombly, R. C. "Organic Living: F. L. Wright's Taliesin Fellowship and Georgi Gurdjieff's Institute for Harmonious Development of Man." *The Wisconsin Magazine of History* 58 (1974-75): 126-139.

Vetterl, Karel. "O Novou Hudbu Pro Rozhlas." *Tempo* 10 (1929): 327-330.

Whitesitt, Linda. "The Role of Women's Music Clubs in Shaping American Concert Life, 1870-1930." Paper presented before the National Meeting of the American Musicological Society, Baltimore, Maryland, November 1988.

"Woodstock." Woodstock Festival. Woodstock, New York: Rotron, Inc., [s.d.].

Wurm, Marie. "Women's Struggle for Recognition in Music." *Etude* 54 (1936): 637, 746.

"Young Pianists Heard." *The New York Times*, 21 November 1916, p. 9.

"Zeisler, Fannie Bloomfield." *Dictionary of American Biography*. New York: Charles Scribner's Sons, 1936, 20: 647-648.

"Zeisler, Fannie Bloomfield." *The National Cyclopedia of American Biography*. New York: James T. White and Co., 1917, 14: 192-193.

Books

Alaya, Flavia. *William Sharp—"Fiona Macleod 1855-1905."* Cambridge, Mass.: Harvard University Press, 1970.

Aldrich, Richard. *Concert Life in New York 1902-1923.* 2d ed. New York: Putnam's Sons, [1941].

Alpers, Anthony. *The Life of Katherine Mansfield*. New York: Viking Press, 1980.

Anderson, Margaret, ed. *The Little Review: Quarterly Journal of Arts and Letters*. Vols. 1-12. New York: March 1914-19 to May 1929, reprint, New York: Kraus Reprint Corp., 1967.

Anderson, Ruth. *Contemporary American Composers*. 2d ed. Boston: G. K. Hall, 1982.

Archer, Gleason. *History of Radio to 1926*. New York: The American Historical Society, 1938.

Auric, Georges. *Quand j'étais là*. Paris: Bernard Grasset, 1979.

Barnouw, Erik. *A Tower in Babel*. Vol. 1, *A History of Broadcasting in the United States*. New York: Oxford University Press, 1966.

Blair, Karen. *The Clubwoman as Feminist: True Womanhood Redefined, 1868-1914*. New York: Homes and Meier, 1980.

Block, Adrienne Fried, and Carol Neuls-Bates. *Women in American Music: A Bibliography of Music and Literature*. Westport, Conn.: Greenwood Press, 1979.

Brody, Elaine. *Paris. The Musical Kaleidoscope 1870-1925*. New York: George Braziller, 1987.

Brubaker, Robert L. *Making Music Chicago Style*. Exhibition Catalogue. Chicago: Chicago Historical Society, 1985.

Butterworth, Neil. *A Dictionary of American Composers*. New York: Garland, 1984.

Chase, Gilbert, ed. *The American Composer Speaks: A Historical Anthology, 1770-1965*. [Baton Rouge]: Louisiana State University Press, 1966.

Copland, Aaron. *The New Music: 1900-1960*. New York: Norton, [1968].

Copland, Aaron, and Vivian Perlis. *Copland: 1900 through 1942*. New York: St. Martin's/Marek, 1984.

Davies, Laurence. *Paths to Modern Music: Aspects of Music from Wagner to the Present Day.* New York: Charles Scribner's Sons, 1971.

Davis, Ronald L. *A History of Music in American Life.* Vol. 3, *The Modern Era, 1920-Present.* Malabar, Florida: Robert Krieger Publishing Co., 1981.

Dickinson, Emily. *The Poems of Emily Dickinson.* Ed. Thomas H. Johnson. Cambridge, Mass.: The Belknap Press of Harvard University Press, 1955.

Dickson, Harry Ellis. *"Gentlemen, More Dolce Please!" (Second Movement). An Irreverent Memoir of Thirty-Five Years in the Boston Symphony Orchestra.* Boston: Beacon Press, 1961.

Douglas, George H. *Women of the 20s.* Dallas, Texas: Saybrook Publishers, 1986.

Duplessis, Rachel Blau. *H.D. The Career of that Struggle.* Bloomington: Indiana University Press, 1986.

Dupree, Mary Herron. "Art Music of the United States during the 1920s: A Study of the Major Issues in Contemporary Periodical Sources." Ph.D. diss., University of Colorado, 1980.

Evers, Alf. *The Catskills, From Wilderness to Woodstock.* Woodstock, New York: The Overlook Press, 1982.

Far, Judith. *The Life and Art of Elinor Wylie.* Baton Rouge: Louisiana State University Press, 1983.

Ffrench, Florence, comp. *Music and Musicians in Chicago.* Chicago, 1899; reprint, New York: Da Capo, 1979.

Flanner, Janet. *Paris Was Yesterday 1925-1939.* New York: Viking, 1927.

Ford, Hugh. *The Left Bank Revisited. Selections from the Paris Tribune, 1917-1934.* University Park: Pennsylvania State University, [1971].

Friedrich, Otto. *Before the Deluge: A Portrait of Berlin in the 1920s.* New York: Harper and Row, 1982.

Gilman, Lawrence. *Edward MacDowell: A Study.* New York: Dodd, Mead, and Co., 1935.

Gray, Thomas A. *Elinor Wylie.* New York: Twayne Publishers, 1969.

Gunther Schuller: A Bio-Bibliography. Bio-Bibliographies in Music, no. 6. Westport, Conn.: Greenwood, 1987.

Gurdjieff: An Annotated Bibliography. Comp. J. Walter Driscoll and the Gurdjieff Foundation of California. New York: Garland Publishing, 1985.

Hahl-Koch, Jelena, ed. *Arnold Schoenberg, Wassily Kandinsky: Letters, Pictures, and Documents.* Trans. by John C. Crawford. London: Faber and Faber, 1984.

Harding, James. *The Ox on the Roof: Scenes from Musical Life in Paris in the Twenties.* London: MacDonald and Co., 1972.

Harlow, Alvin F. *Old Wires and New Waves: The History of the Telegraph, Telephone, and Wireless.* New York: 1936; reprint, New York: Arno Press, 1971.

Head, Sydney W. *Broadcasting in America.* Boston: Houghton Mifflin Co., 1956.

Heinsheimer, Hans W. *Best Regards to Aida: The Defeats and Victories of a Music Man on Two Continents.* New York: Alfred A. Knopf, 1968.

Hitchcock, H. Wiley. *Music in the United States.* 3d ed. Englewood Cliffs, New Jersey: Prentice-Hall, 1988.

Hoover, Kathleen, and John Cage. *Virgil Thomson: His Life and Music.* New York: Thomas Yoseloff, 1959.

Horn, David. *The Literature of American Music in Books and Folk Music Collections: A Fully Annotated Bibliography.* Metuchen, New Jersey: Scarecrow Press, 1977.

Howard, John Tasker. *Our American Music. Three Hundred Years of It.* 3d ed. New York: Thomas Y. Crowell Co., 1954.

Howe, Mark Anthony De Wolfe. *The Boston Symphony Orchestra 1881-1931.* Semicentennial edition. Revised and extended in collaboration with John Burk. Boston: 1914; reprint, New York: Da Capo, 1978.

Hoyt, Nancy. *Elinor Wylie. The Portrait of an Unknown Lady.* New York: Bobbs-Merrill Co., 1935.

Ireland, Norma Olin. *Index to Women of the World from Ancient to Modern Times: Biographies and Portraits.* Westwood, Mass.: F. W. Faxon and Co., 1970; Supplement; Metuchen, New Jersey: Scarecrow Press, 1988.

Jacobs, Herbert Austin. *Frank Lloyd Wright, America's Greatest Architect.* New York: Harcourt, Brace and World, 1965.

Johnson, E. A. "The Chicago Orchestra 1891-1942." Ph.D. diss., University of Chicago, 1951.

Klauber-Friedman, Ruth. *The History of Musicians Club of Women.* 2 vols. Chicago: Privately printed, 1975.

Krummel, Donald. *Bibliographical Handbook of American Music.* Urbana: University of Illinois Press, 1987.

_____. *Resources of American Music History: A Directory of Source Materials from Colonial Times to World War II.* Urbana: University of Illinois Press, 1981.

The League of Composers: A Record of Performances and a Survey of General Activities from 1923 to 1935. New York: The League of Composers, [n.d.].

Leichtentritt, Hugo. *Serge Koussevitzky, the Boston Symphony Orchestra, and the New American Music.* Cambridge, Mass.: Harvard University Press, 1946.

Levy, Alan Howard. *Musical Nationalism. American Composers' Search for Identity.* Contributions in American Studies, no. 66. Westport, Conn.: Greenwood Press, 1983.

Lowens, Marjorie. "The New York Years of Edward MacDowell." Ph.D. diss., University of Michigan, 1971.

Meetings with Remarkable Men. Film directed by Peter Brook. Music adapted and compiled by Laurence Rosenthal. 1978.

Mooser, Robert-Aloys. *Regards sur la musique contemporaine 1921-1946.* Préface d'Arthur Honegger. Lausanne: Librairie F. Rouge et Cie., S.A., 1946.

Mueser, Barbara. "The Criticism of New Music in New York, 1919-1929." Ph.D. diss., City University of New York, 1975.

Olin Downes on Music. A Selection from his Writings during the Half-Century 1906 to 1955. Ed. Irene Downes. New York: Simon and Schuster, 1957.

Olson, Stanley. *Elinor Wylie. A Life Apart.* New York: The Dial Press, 1979.

Orage, A. R. *The Active Mind. Adventures in Awareness.* New York: Hermitage House, 1954.

_____, ed. *Psychological Exercises.* New York: Farrar and Rinehart, Inc., [1930].

Otis, Philo Adams. *The Chicago Symphony Orchestra. Its Organization, Growth, and Development (1891-1924).* Chicago: Clayton F. Summy, [1924].

Pawley, Edward. *BBC Engineering 1922-1972.* London: BBC Publications, 1972.

Perlis, Vivian. *Two Men for Modern Music. E. Robert Schmitz and Herman Langinger.* I.S.A.M. Monographs, no. 9. Brooklyn, N.Y.: Institute for Studies of American Music, 1978.

Pro musica Quarterly (New York). September 1923-October 1929.

Quinn, Vincent G. *Hilda Doolittle (H. D.).* New York: Twayne Publishers, 1967.

Robinson, Janice S. *H. D. The Life and Work of an American Poet.* Boston: Houghton Mifflin Co., 1982.

Rosenfeld, Paul. *An Hour with American Music.* London: J. B. Lippincott Company, 1929.

_____. *Musical Chronicle (1917-1923).* New York: Harcourt, Brace, and Company, [1923].

Rowe, Mike. *Chicago Breakdown.* London: Eddison Press Ltd., 1973.

Schickel, Richard. *The World of Carnegie Hall.* New York: Julian Messner, Inc., 1960.

Scott, Anne Firor. *Making the Invisible Woman Visible.* Urbana and Chicago: University of Illinois Press, 1984.

Shanet, Howard. *Philharmonic. A History of New York's Orchestra.* New York: Doubleday and Co., Inc., 1975.

Sharp, William. *The Writings of "Fiona Macleod."* Uniform ed. Arranged by Mrs. William Sharp. New York: 1895 and 1909. Facsimile ed., Ann Arbor, Michigan: 1972.

Shattuck, Roger. *The Banquet Years, the Arts in France 1885-1918: Alfred Jarry, Henri Rousseau, Erik Satie, Guillaume Apollinaire.* New York: Harcourt, Brace, Janovich, 1958.

Shead, Richard. *Music in the 1920s.* London: Duckworth, 1976.

Shirer, William. *Twentieth-Century Journey: A Memoir of a Life and Times.* New York: Simon and Schuster, 1976.

60th Season Maverick Sunday Concerts. [Woodstock, New York]: Maverick Concerts, Inc., 1975.

Solow, Linda I., ed. *The Boston Composers Projects: A Bibliography of Contemporary Music.* Cambridge, Mass.: MIT Press, 1983.

Thomson, Virgil. *Music Right and Left.* New York: Henry Holt and Co., 1951.

Tyler, Parker. *The Divine Comedy of Pavel Tchelitchew. A Biography.* New York: Fleet Publishing Co., 1967.

U.S. War Department. *War Department Annual Reports, 1918.* [Report of the Chief Signal Officer]. Vol. I. Washington, D.C.: Government Printing Office, 1919.

Varèse, Louise. *Varèse. A Looking-Glass Diary. Volume I: 1883-1928.* New York: W. W. Norton, 1972.

Weiss, Piero, and Richard Taruskin, eds. *Music in the Western World. A History in Documents.* New York: Schirmer Books, 1984.

William Sharp (Fiona Macleod) A Memoir. Compiled by his wife Elizabeth A. Sharp. London: William Heinemann, 1910.

Women in Music. Vol. 47, *The Etude Music Magazine*, 1929.

Women in Particular: An Index to American Women. Phoenix, Arizona: Oryx Press, 1984.

Women of Achievement. New York: House of Field, 1940.

Wylie, Elinor. *Collected Poems.* New York: Alfred A. Knopf, 1932.

Music

Manuscripts

Antheil, George. Fourth Sonata for Piano, "Jazz" Sonata. Berlin: March 23, 1923. Inscribed "For Carol Robinson." Piano solo. GU MS 300. This work is the same minus a few details as the Sonata for Piano below and differs completely from the Fourth Piano Sonata published by Weintraub in 1951.

_____. A Jazz Symphony. To Evelyn Friede. 1925. For 4 saxophones, 2 clarinets (three players), 2 oboes, 3 trumpets, 3 trombones, 1 tuba, 2 banjos, xylophone, percussion, strings. Antheil Estate, c/o Charles Amirkhanian, El Cerrito, California.

_____. A Jazz Symphony. 1925. Piano reduction. DLC, George Antheil, Holograph Music Manuscripts, Music 3149, reel 1, item #13. Photocopy of the holograph, Antheil Estate.

_____. Sonata for Piano. [A roman numeral is marked through, and the nickname "Jazz Sonata" below has the word "Jazz" crossed out. Another hand has added above this title "Jazz Sonata 1922," identified by Whitesitt as Boski Antheil's writing.] Piano solo. Antheil Estate.

Ives, Charles E. Second Sonata for Violin and Piano. Ed. John Kirkpatrick. GU MS 300. Photostatic copy, of CtY, Charles Ives MS, Kirkpatrick no. 5.

_____. Sonata #3 for Piano and Violin. GU MS 300. Photostatic copy of CtY, Charles Ives MS, Kirkpatrick no. 6.

Martinů, Bohuslav. Par T.S.F. GU MS 300. For a facsimile and description of the manuscript, see Bohuslav Martinů, *Par T.S.F.* Ed. Glenda Dawn Goss. Prague: Panton Press, 1990.

Weidig, Adolf. Canzonetta. "For Carol Robinson." Transcribed for two pianos by Orvis Ross. GU MS 300.

Printed Scores

Antheil, George. *Five Songs 1919-1920 for Soprano and Piano.* After Adelaide Crapsey. Cos-Cob Press, 1934; copyright renewed and assigned to Boosey and Hawkes, 1961.

_____. *Sonata for Piano* ("Airplane Sonata"). Together with extracts from other Antheil works, in *This Quarter* no. 2, Antheil Musical Supplement, ed. Ernest Walsh and Ethel Moorhead. Milan, Italy: Il convegnio, [1925].

_____. *Sonata no. 4 for Piano.* New York: Weintraub Music Co., 1951.

Cowell, Henry. "Aeolian Harp." In *Piano Music by Henry Cowell.* New York: Associated Music Publishers, 1960.

_____. "How Old is Song?" Words by Harry Cowell, music by
    Henry Cowell. Brooklyn, N.Y.: The Ernest Williams School of
    Music, [1943].

_____. *Sonata for Violin and Piano*. New York: Associated Music
    Publishers, 1947.

Harris, Roy. *Sonata for Violin and Piano*. Revised edition. New York:
    Belwin-Mills, [1974].

Hartmann, Thomas de. *Musique pour les mouvements de G. I. Gurdjieff*.
    Paris: Editions Janus, 1950.

Ives, Charles. *Third Sonata for Piano and Violin*. Ed. Sol Babitz and
    Ingolf Dahl. Bryn Mawr, Pa.: Merion Music, Inc., 1951.

MacDowell, Edward. *Piano Pieces (Opp. 51, 55, 61, 52)*. Introduction
    by H. Wiley Hitchcock. Earlier American Music, 8. New York:
    Da Capo Press, 1972.

_____. *Piano Sonatas*. New York: Schirmer, 1984.

A Treasury of American Song. 2d ed. Text by Olin Downes and Elie
    Siegmeister. Music arranged by Elie Siegmeister. New York:
    Alfred A. Knopf, 1940.

Walker, William. *The Southern Harmony & Musical Companion*, 1854.
    Facsimile edition, ed. Glenn C. Wilcox. Lexington, Kentucky:
    The University Press of Kentucky, 1987.

George Antheil: Selected Books and Articles

Adams, Stephen. "Musical Neofism: Pound's Theory of Harmony in
    Context." *Mosaic* 13 (1980): 46-49.

"Antheil Art Bursts on Startled Ears." *The New York Times*, 11 April
    1927, p. 23.

Copland, Aaron. "George Antheil." *Modern Music* 2 (1925): 26-28.

Douglas, John R. "The Composer and his Music on Record." *Library Journal* 92 (1967): 1117-1121.

Ford, Hugh. *Four Lives in Paris*. With Foreword by Glenway Wescott. San Francisco: North Point Press, 1987.

Gilman, Lawrence. "An Afternoon with the Younger Generation, American and European." *New York Herald Tribune*, 17 November 1924, p. 12.

Imbs, Bravig. *Confessions of Another Young Man*. New York: The Henkle-Yewdale House, Inc., 1936.

McAlmon, Robert. *Being Geniuses Together, 1920-1930*. Revised with supplementary chapters by Kay Boyle. New York: Doubleday & Company, 1968.

Morton, Brian. *Americans in Paris: An Anecdotal Street Guide*. Ann Arbor, Michigan: Olivia and Hill Press, 1984.

Perlis, Vivian. "The Futurist Music of Leo Ornstein." *Notes* 31 (1975): 735-750.

Pound, Ezra. *Antheil and the Treatise on Harmony*. Chicago: 1927; repr., with a new introduction by Ned Rorem; New York: Da Capo, 1968.

Shirley, Wayne D. "Another American in Paris: George Antheil's Correspondence with Mary Curtis Bok." *The Quarterly Journal of the Library of Congress* 34 (1977): 2-22.

Thompson, Randall. "American Composers V. George Antheil." *Modern Music* 8 (1931): 17-27.

Whitesitt, Linda. *The Life and Music of George Antheil (1900-1959)*. Ann Arbor, Michigan: UMI Research Press, 1983.

_____, and Charles Amirkhanian. "Antheil, George." *The New Grove Dictionary of American Music*. Ed. H. Wiley Hitchcock and Stanley Sadie. London: Macmillan, 1986, 1: 51-55.

Henry Cowell: Selected Books and Articles

Lichtenwanger, William. *The Music of Henry Cowell, A Descriptive Catalogue*. I.S.A.M. Monographs, no. 23. Brooklyn, N.Y.: Institute for Studies in American Music, 1986.

Manion, Martha L. *Writings About Henry Cowell. An Annotated Bibliography*. I.S.A.M. Monographs, no. 16. Brooklyn, N.Y.: Institute for Studies in American Music, 1986.

Mead, Rita H. *Henry Cowell's New Music 1925-1936. The Society, the Music Editions, and the Recordings*. Ann Arbor, Michigan: UMI Research Press, 1981.

_____. "Henry Cowell's New Music Society." *Journal of Musicology* 1 (1982): 449-463.

Persichetti, Vincent. "Reviews of Records: Modern American Music Series, Columbia Masterworks." *Musical Quarterly* 40 (1954): 471-476.

Saylor, Bruce. *The Writings of Henry Cowell: A Descriptive Catalogue*. I.S.A.M. Monographs, no. 7. Brooklyn, N.Y.: Institute of Studies in American Music, 1977.

_____, and William Lichtenwanger, with Elizabeth A. Wright. "Cowell, Henry." *The New Grove Dictionary of American Music*. Ed. by H. Wiley Hitchcock and Stanley Sadie. London: Macmillan, 1986, 1: 520-529.

Weisgall, Hugo. "The Music of Henry Cowell." *Musical Quarterly* 45 (1959): 484-507.

Roy Harris: Selected Books and Articles

Cowell, Henry, ed. "Roy Harris." Chap. in *American Composers on American Music, a Symposium*. [Stanford University, Ca.]: Stanford University Press, 1933.

Farwell, Arthur. "Roy Harris." *Musical Quarterly* 18 (1932): 18-32.

Harris, Roy. "The Growth of a Composer." *Musical Quarterly* 29 (1934): 188-191.

_____. "Problems of American Composers." *The American Composer Speaks*, ed. Gilbert Chase. [Baton Rouge]: Louisiana State University Press, 1966.

Levy, Alan Howard. "Roy Harris and Strident Americanism." Chap. in *Musical Nationalism. American Composers' Search for Identity.* Contributions in American Studies, no. 66. Westport, Conn.: Greenwood Press, 1983.

Slonimsky, Nicolas. "Roy Harris." *Musical Quarterly* 33 (1947): 17-37.

Stehman, Dan. "Roy Harris." *The New Grove Dictionary of American Music.* Ed. H. Wiley Hitchcock and Stanley Sadie. London: Macmillan, 1986, 2: 331-336.

_____. *Roy Harris: An American Musical Pioneer.* Boston, Mass.: Twayne Publishers, 1984.

Straussburg, Robert, comp. *Roy Harris, A Catalog of His Works.* Los Angeles: California State University, 1973.

Charles Ives: Selected Books and Articles

Block, Geoffrey. *Charles Ives. A Bio-Bibliography.* Bio-Bibliographies in Music, no. 14. Westport, Conn.: Greenwood Press, 1988.

Burkholder, J. Peter. "Charles Ives and His Father: A Response to Maynard Solomon." *I.S.A.M. Newsletter* 18 (1988): 8-11.

_____. *Charles Ives: the Ideas Behind the Music.* New Haven: Yale University Press, 1985.

_____. "Quotation and Emulation: Charles Ives's Uses of His Models." *Musical Quarterly* 71 (1985): 1-26.

Cowell, Henry. "Review of Records. Ives: Sonatas Nos. 1 and 3." *Musical Quarterly* 39 (1953): 323-325.

De Lerma, Dominique-René. *Charles Edward Ives, 1874-1954: A Bibliography of His Music.* Kent, Ohio: Kent State University Press, 1970.

Gibbens, John Jeffrey. "Debussy's Impact on Ives: An Assessment." D.M.A. diss., University of Illinois at Urbana-Champaigne, 1985.

Hitchcock, H. Wiley. *Ives.* London: Oxford University Press, 1977.

Ives, Charles E. *Memos.* Ed. John Kirkpatrick. New York: W. W. Norton, 1982.

Kirkpatrick, John. "Ives, Charles." *The New Grove Dictionary of American Music.* Ed. by H. Wiley Hitchcock and Stanley Sadie. London: Macmillan, 1986, 2: 503-520.

_____, comp. "A Temporary Mimeographed Catalogue of the Music Manuscripts and Related Materials of Charles Edward Ives, 1874-1954, Given by Mrs. Ives to the Library of the Yale School of Music, September 1955." [New Haven]: Library of the Yale School of Music, 1960.

Mead, Rita H. "Cowell, Ives, and New Music." *Musical Quarterly* 66 (1980): 538-599.

Perkins, L. "The Violin Sonatas by Charles Ives." D.M.A. diss., The Eastman School, 1961.

Perlis, Vivian. *Charles Ives Remembered. An Oral History.* New Haven, Conn.: Yale University Press, 1974.

Phillips, Harvey E. Notes for *Charles Ives Complete Chamber Music,* vol. 1. Vox Records, SVBX 564.

Rossiter, Frank R. *Charles Ives and his America.* New York: Liveright, 1975.

Solomon, Maynard. "Charles Ives: Some Questions of Veracity." *Journal of the American Musicological Society* 40 (1987): 443-70.

Bohuslav Martinů: Selected Books and Articles

Clapham, John. "Martinů's Instrumental Style." *Music Review* 24 (1963): 158-167.

Downes, Olin. "Martinů at 60." *The New York Times*, 7 January 1951, sect. 2, p. 7.

Ferroud, Pierre Octave. "A Great Musician of Today, Bohuslav Martinů." *The Chesterian* 18/132 (1937): 89-93.

Goss, Glenda Dawn. "Bohuslav Martinů et la T.S.F." In *Actes du Colloque: Martinů et la France 24-27 avril 1990.* Vanves, France: Mouvement Janáček, Cahier numéro spécial 11 (1990): 33-37.

_____. "Martinů Resources at the University of Georgia." Paper presented before the International Conference and Festival Martinů and the 20th Century, St. Louis, Missouri, 24 October 1990.

Halbreich, Harry. *Bohuslav Martinů*. Zurich: Atlantis, 1968.

_____. *Bohuslav Martinů, Werkverzeichnis, Dokumentation und Biographie.* Zurich: Atlantis Verlag, 1968.

Hinson, Maurice. "Bohuslav Martinů-Czechoslovakia's Greatest 20th Century Composer." *Clavier* 21 (1982): 19-24.

Hirsbrunner, Theo. "Bohuslav Martinu: Die Soloklavierwerke der Dreissiger Jahre." *Archiv für Musikwissenschaft* 39 (1982): 64-77.

Hoerée, Arthur. "La technique de piano d'Albert Roussel." *La Revue musicale* 10, Supplement (1928-29): 84-103.

Kuna, Milan. "Korespondence Bohuslava Martinů Václavu Talichovi 1924-1939." *HudVéda* 7 (1970): 212-247.

Large, Brian. *Martinů*. New York: Holmes and Meier, 1975.

_____. "Martinů, Bohuslav." *The New Grove Dictionary of Music and Musicians.* Ed. Stanley Sadie. London: Macmillan, 1980, 11: 731-735.

Lowenbach, Jan. "Czechoslovak Composers and Musicians in America."
    Musical Quarterly 29 (1943): 313-328.

Martinů, Bohuslav. "Artists are Citizens." *Modern Music* 22 (1944): 10-
    11.

_____. "Témoignage tchécoslovaque." *La Revue musicale* 18 (1937):
    366.

Martinů, Charlotte. *My Life with Bohuslav Martinů.* Trans. Diderik D.
    De Jong. Prague: Orbis Press Agency, 1978.

Mihule, Jaroslav. *Bohuslav Martinů.* Prague: Agence du Presse Orbis,
    1979.

Šafránek, Milos. "Bohuslav Martinů." *Musical Quarterly* 29 (1943):
    329-354.

_____. *Bohuslav Martinů. His Life and Works.* Trans. Roberta
    Finlayson-Samsourova. London: Allan Wingate, 1961.

                    Writings by Carol Robinson's Friends

Anderson, Margaret. *The Fiery Fountains.* New York: Hermitage
    House, [1951].

_____. *The "Little Review" Anthology.* New York: Horizon Press,
    1953.

_____. *My Thirty Years' War. An Autobiography.* Covici, Friede
    Publishers, 1930.

_____. *The Strange Necessity. An Autobiography; Resolutions and
    Reminiscences to 1969.* New York: Horizon Press, 1969.

_____. *The Unknowable Gurdjieff.* New York: Samuel Weiser,
    [1962].

Antheil, George. "Abstraction and Time in Music." *The Little Review*
    (Autumn-Winter 1924-1925): 13-35.

_____. *Bad Boy of Music*. Garden City, N.Y.: 1945; reprint, with a new introduction by Charles Amirkhanian. New York: Da Capo, 1981.

Caruso, Dorothy Park. *Dorothy Caruso, A Personal History*. New York: Hermitage House, 1952.

Cowell, Henry and Sidney Cowell. *Charles Ives and His Music*. New York: Oxford University Press, 1955.

[Doolittle, Hilda]. *Collected Poems of H. D.* New York: Liveright Publishing Corp., 1925. Sixth printing, 1940.

Gurdjieff, Georgi. *Views from the Real World. Early Talks in Moscow, Essentuki, Tiflis, Berlin, London, Paris, New York, and Chicago As Recollected by His Pupils*. With a Foreword by Jeanne de Salzmann. New York: E. P. Dutton & Co., 1973.

H. D. [Hilda Doolittle]. *End to Torment: A Memoir of Ezra Pound*. Ed. by Norman Homes Pearson and Michael King. With poems from "Hilda's Book" by Ezra Pound. New York: New Directions Publishing Corp., 1979.

H. D., Collected Poems, 1912-1944. Ed. Louis L. Martz. New York: A New Directions Book, 1983.

Hartmann, Thomas de. *Our Life with Mr. Gurdjieff*. New York: Cooper Square Publishers, Inc., 1964.

Hemingway, Ernest. [Untitled article in] *The Transatlantic Review* 2 (1924): 341-342.

Leblanc, Georgette. *Souvenirs; My Life with Maeterlinck*. Trans. Janet Flanner. New York: Dutton, [1932].

Munson, Gorham. *The Awakening Twenties*. Baton Rouge: Louisiana State University Press, 1985.

Pound, Ezra, and *The Little Review*. *The Letters of Ezra Pound to Margaret Anderson: The Little Review Correspondence*. Ed. Thomas L. Scott & Melvin J. Friedman, with the assistance of Jackson R. Bryer. New York: A New Directions Book, 1988.

Welch, Louise. *Orage with Gurdjieff in America*. Boston: Routledge and Kegan Paul, 1982.

Wright, Frank Lloyd. *An Autobiography*. New York: Horizon Press, 1977.

Wright, Olgivanna Lloyd. *Frank Lloyd Wright, His Life, His Work, His Words*. New York: Horizon Press, 1966.

Interviews and Correspondence with
Friends, Family and Pupils of Carol Robinson

Interview with Eleanor Anderson, pupil, 1988.

Telephone conversation with Robert Bowman, concert pianist, 1988.

Telephone conversation with Madeleine Carabo-Cone, violinist, 1987.

Telephone conversation with Marjorie Corbett, pupil, 1988.

Telephone conversation with Sidney Cowell (Mrs. Henry Cowell), 1989.

Interviews and telephone conversations with Elizabeth Delza (Mrs. Gorham Munson), dancer, choreographer, and friend, 1987-1992.

Telephone conversation and correspondence with Sister Francis Assisi, the Convent of the Sisters of St. Francis, Oldenburg, Indiana, 1988.

Telephone conversation with Lois Baptiste Hausch, pupil of Fannie Bloomfield Zeisler contemporary with Carol Robinson, 1989.

Telephone conversation with John Hill, Taliesin Fellowship, 1989.

Telephone conversation with Dushka Howarth, 1988.

Telephone conversation with Sister Mary George, Rosemont College, 1988.

Telephone conversation and correspondence with Millie Morganstern, pupil and friend, 1988.

Telephone conversations and correspondence with Lawrence Morris, friend, 1988.

Telephone conversations and correspondence with David Robinson, Robinson's nephew, 1988-1991.

Telephone conversation with Laurence Rosenthal, composer, 1988.

Telephone conversation with John Schlenk, pianist for Delza dance classes, 1989.

Telephone conversation with Hilda Schuster, Dalcroze School, 1988.

Telephone conversations and correspondence with Phoebe Sells, Robinson's niece, 1988-1991.

Telephone conversations and correspondence with Julie Steinberg, pupil and concert pianist, 1988-1991.

Telephone conversation and interview with Laura Steinberg, pupil, 1988.

Telephone conversations and interviews with Millie Steinberg, pupil and friend, 1988-1990.

Telephone conversation with Mrs. Halsey Stevens, 1989.

Correspondence with Harriet Todd, friend and pianist, 1989.

Telephone conversations with Louise Welch, friend and author of *Orage with Gurdjieff in America*, 1988.

Telephone conversation with Dr. William Welch, friend, 1988.

Telephone conversation with Iovanna Wright, pupil and daughter of Frank Lloyd Wright, 1989.

Correspondence with Sister M. Vivian Ivantic, St. Scholastic Priory, Chicago, 1989.

Correspondence with Marion Morrey Richter, fellow pianist in 1927 performance of Antheil's *Ballet mécanique*, 1989.

Correspondence with Genia Robinor, friend, president of the Leschetizky Association, 1988.

Correspondence with Mrs. Powell Weaver, friend, 1988.

Correspondence with Ivri Patricia Wormser, friend and neighbor, 1989.

Index

Composers in Appendix A, Robinson's performing repertory, as well as Robinson's own works in Appendix B are omitted from the Index. Names in the first instance are already listed alphabetically, while in the second, the works may be located through the Table of Contents.

ABOUT THE AUTHOR

GLENDA DAWN GOSS (B.A. *magna cum laude*, Phi Beta Kappa, University of Georgia; Certificate, Université libre de Bruxelles; Ph.D., University of North Carolina, Chapel Hill) teaches music history and musicology at the University of Georgia. She also heads the Musicology Division and is active as a guest lecturer and pianist. An editor of Renaissance music, Dr. Goss published various articles in professional journals on music at the Habsburg court of Mary of Hungary before turning her attention to the twentieth century. In the Hargrett Library at the University of Georgia, she has worked with several twentieth-century collections including the Carol Robinson Collection and the Olin Downes Papers. She has edited and performed music from the Carol Robinson Collection, much of which appears in the present volume for the first time.